THE BIBLE

SMOOTHIE

RECIPES

3 in 1

+150 recipes to Lose Weight, Detoxify, Fight Disease, and Live Long

Vincent Moore, Donnie King, Jennifer Abrahams

Sommario

Top 50 Amazing SMOOTHIE Recipes 11

Lose Weight, Detoxify, Fight Disease, and Live Long 11

INTRODUCTION 13

1.TROPICAL PINA COLADA SMOOTHIE.............................. 14

2.STRAWBERRY PROTEIN SHAKE 16

3.HEALTHY CHOCOLATE PEANUT BUTTER SMOOTHIE 18

4.STRAWBERRY PINEAPPLE SMOOTHIE............................. 20

5.STRAWBERRY BANANA SPINACH SMOOTHIE 22

6.LAYERED CHOCOLATE BANANA SMOOTHIE WITH PROTEIN.. 25

7.TROPICAL SPINACH SMOOTHIE 28

8.REFRESHING GINGER PINEAPPLE SMOOTHIE 30

9.THE BEST GREEN SMOOTHIE RECIPES 32

10.SUPERFOOD PROTEIN SMOOTHIE.................................. 34

11.PEANUT BUTTER BANANA COLD BREW PROTEIN SMOOTHIE.. 36

12... 38

INGREDIENTS 38

13.SWEET CHERRY ALMOND SMOOTHIE 40

14.LOVELY GREENS SMOOTHIE... 42

15.CHOCOLATE POWERHOUSE SMOOTHIE:.......................... 44

16.YOUTHFUL GLOW GREEN SMOOTHIE:............................ 46

17.PEACHY MANGO SMOOTHIE 48

3

18.BEST PUMPKIN PANCAKES RECIPE 50

19.BREAKFAST SUPER-SHAKE 53

20.TWO-MINUTE BREAKFAST SMOOTHIE 55

21.STRAWBERRY GREEN GODDESS SMOOTHIE 57

22.STRAWBERRY SMOOTHIE 59

23.RASPBERRY AND APPLE SMOOTHIE 61

24.CARROT AND ORANGE SMOOTHIE 63

25.SUNSHINE SMOOTHIE 65

26.BANANA SMOOTHIE 67

28.MANGO LASSI 69

29.KALE SMOOTHIE 71

30.CHERRY SMOOTHIE 73

31.COCONUT & BANANA SMOOTHIE 75

32.TURMERIC SMOOTHIE BOWL 77

33.KEFIR BREAKFAST SMOOTHIE 79

34.VEGAN SMOOTHIE 81

35.CREAMY MANGO & COCONUT SMOOTHIE 83

36.PEACH MELBA SMOOTHIE 85

37.SUPER BERRY SMOOTHIE 87

38.CRANBERRY & RASPBERRY SMOOTHIE 89

39.MANGO & BANANA SMOOTHIE 91

40.STRAWBERRY BREAKFAST SMOOTHIE 93

41.TROPICAL BREAKFAST SMOOTHIE 95

42.BANANA, CLEMENTINE & MANGO SMOOTHIE 97

43.FOREST FRUIT & BANANA SMOOTHIE 99

44.SMOOTHIE JELLIES WITH ICE CREAM...........................101

45.SMOOTHIE CUBES 103

46.GREEN GODDESS SMOOTHIE BOWL 105

47.VITAMIN BOOSTER SMOOTHIE 109

48.AVOCADO SMOOTHIE...111

49.HEART HELPER SMOOTHIE...113

50.AVOCADO & STRAWBERRY SMOOTHIE.........................115

CONCLUSION 117

The Super Healthy Smoothie recipes.......................118

50 Essential Smoothies to Get Healthy 118

INTRODUCTION 120

1.TAHINI DATE AND CINNAMON SMOOTHIE.....................121

2.SWEET POTATO SMOOTHIE BOWL [TASTES LIKE SWEET POTATO PIE!] 123

3.MATCHA MINT COCONUT SMOOTHIE BOWL 125

4.YOGA GLOW SMOOTHIE + MY NEW MORNING ROUTINE 127

5.ALMOND CHAI GREEN SMOOTHIE 129

6.BLUEBERRY GREEN SMOOTHIE BOWL 131

7.PINEAPPLE MOJITO GREEN SMOOTHIE 133

8.MANGO ALMOND BUTTER SMOOTHIE..............................135

9.CARROT CAKE SMOOTHIE BOWL 137

10.HOLIDAY DETOX GREEN APPLE SMOOTHIE 139

11.HONEY AND WILD BLUEBERRY SMOOTHIE 141

12.BERRY GREEN SMOOTHIE 143

13.SIMPLE COCONUT GREEN SMOOTHIE 145

14. WORLD'S BEST WATERMELON SMOOTHIE 147

15.MANGO SMOOTHIE RECIPE 149

16.GOJI PEACH CHERRY SMOOTHIE 151

17.CHAI-SPICED STRAWBERRY MANGO SMOOTHIE 153

18.BLUEBERRY COCONUT WATER SMOOTHIE 155

19.ANTI-INFLAMMATORY TURMERIC SMOOTHIE 157

20.KETO GREEN SMOOTHIE 159

21.CHOCOLATE PEANUT BUTTER BANANA SMOOTHIE.161

22.BLUE SMOOTHIE 163

23.DRAGON FRUIT SMOOTHIE 165

24.AVOCADO SPINACH SMOOTHIE 167

25.BANANA SMOOTHIE 169

26.STRAWBERRY BLUEBERRY SMOOTHIE 171

27.PEACH SMOOTHIE 173

28.WATERMELON SMOOTHIE 175

29.BLUEBERRY SMOOTHIE 177

30.STRAWBERRY OATMEAL SMOOTHIE 179

31.PEACH RASPBERRY SMOOTHIE 181

32.SECRET INGREDIENT HEALTHY SMOOTHIE 183

33.BLACKBERRY LIME SMOOTHIE 185

34.PINEAPPLE COCONUT SMOOTHIE 187

35.CHOCOLATE RASPBERRY SMOOTHIE 189

36.RASPBERRY COCONUT SMOOTHIE 191

37.GREEN SMOOTHIE BOWL 193

39.DRAGONFRUIT SMOOTHIE PITAYA BOWL 197

40.TROPICAL COCONUT SMOOTHIE BOWL 199

41.BERRY ALMOND SMOOTHIE BOWL.............................201

42.SIMPLE PALEO GRANOLA 203

43.TROPICALE SMOOTHIE 205

44.RASPBERRY PEACH SPINACH SMOOTHIE....................207

45.BANANA PEANUT BUTTER AND DATE SMOOTHIE 209

46.PITAYA SMOOTHIE BOWL 211

47.MIXED BERRY SMOOTHIE BOWL 213

48.PEACHY GREEN SMOOTHIE 215

49.GREEN MONSTER SMOOTHIE 217

50.LIGHTENED-UP DAIRY-FREE ORANGE SMOOTHIE 219

CONCLUSION 221

The Smoothie Recipe Book for Beginners 222

50 Smoothie Recipes..................................222

INTRODUCTION 224

1.MINTY PINEAPPLE SMOOTHIE 225

2.GREEN RAINBOW SMOOTHIE BOWL 227

3.TROPICAL SMOOTHIE BOWL.............................229

4.TURMERIC SMOOTHIE BOWL 231

5. CREAMY MANGO & COCONUT SMOOTHIE 233

6.SUPER BERRY SMOOTHIE.................................235

7.BLACKBERRY & BEETROOT SMOOTHIE 237

8.VITAMIN BOOSTER SMOOTHIE................................239

9.BERRY SMOOTHIE CUBES................................241

10.PEACH MELBA SMOOTHIE 243

11.BANANA, CLEMENTINE & MANGO SMOOTHIE...........245

12.AÇAÍ SMOOTHIE 247

13.MANGO & PASSION FRUIT SMOOTHIE........................249

14.FOREST FRUIT & BANANA SMOOTHIE 251

15.SMOOTHIE JELLIES WITH ICE CREAM................253

16.BANANA, HONEY & HAZELNUT SMOOTHIE 255

17.BREAKFAST SUPER-SHAKE 257

18.ALMOND MILK 259

19.EASY CHOCOLATE FUDGE CAKE................................261

20.FAUX GRAS WITH TOAST & PICKLES........................264

21.STRAWBERRY ACAI SMOOTHIE................................267

22.POST WORKOUT GREEN SMOOTHIE 269

23.SPICED PERSIMMON SMOOTHIE 271

24.GOLDEN BEET, CARROT AND TURMERIC SMOOTHIE.273

25.CHOCOLATE COLLAGEN SMOOTHIE 275

26.CASHEW DATE SHAKE (VEGAN, PALEO)................277

27.DARK CHERRY SMOOTHIE BOWL 279

28.PITAYA SMOOTHIE BOWL 281

29.HEALTHY COCOA, BANANA, PB SMOOTHIE 283

30.TURMERIC LATTE..285

31.FRUIT & YOGURT SMOOTHIE.........................287

32.UNICORN SMOOTHIE.....................................289

33.CHOCOLATE-BANANA PROTEIN SMOOTHIE.............292

34.CREAMSICLE BREAKFAST SMOOTHIE.......................294

35.BERRY-COCONUT SMOOTHIE.........................296

36.CARROT SMOOTHIE.....................................298

37.HONEYDEW SMOOTHIE BOWL.........................300

38.PEANUT BUTTER & JELLY SMOOTHIE.......................302

39.CANTALOUPE SMOOTHIE BOWL....................304

40.JASON MRAZ'S AVOCADO GREEN SMOOTHIE.............306

41.TOFU TROPIC SMOOTHIE.............................308

42.GOOD GREEN TEA SMOOTHIE.........................310

43.ORANGE FLAX SMOOTHIE.............................312

44.MERMAID SMOOTHIE BOWL..........................314

45.ALMOND-MATCHA GREEN SMOOTHIE BOWL.............316

46.UNICORN SMOOTHIE.....................................318

47.TRIPLE MELON SMOOTHIE.............................321

48.CITRUS BERRY SMOOTHIE.............................323

49.WATERMELON-TURMERIC SMOOTHIE.......................325

50.REALLY GREEN SMOOTHIE.............................327

CONCLUSION..329

Top 50 Amazing SMOOTHIE Recipes

Lose Weight, Detoxify, Fight Disease, and Live Long

Vincent Moore

All rights reserved.

Disclaimer

INTRODUCTION

A smoothie recipe is a drink made from pureed raw fruit and/or vegetables, using a blender. A smoothie often has a liquid base such as water, fruit juice, dairy products, such as milk, yogurt, ice cream or cottage cheese.

1.TROPICAL PINA COLADA SMOOTHIE

INGREDIENTS

- ❖ 1 16 oz. bag Season's Choice Tropical Blend Frozen Fruit

- ❖ 1 15 oz. can lite coconut milk

- ❖ 1 teaspoon Stone mill Pure Vanilla Extract

- ❖ Optional toppings: Millville Oats and Honey Granola, unsweetened coconut flakes, fresh blueberries, fresh pineapple slice

INSTRUCTIONS

1. Place frozen tropical fruit, coconut milk, and vanilla extract in your Ambiano Professional Nutrition Blender. Blend until smooth*.

2. Add optional toppings as desired, i.e., Millville Oats and Honey Granola, unsweetened coconut flakes, fresh blueberries, and a fresh pineapple slice

2.STRAWBERRY PROTEIN SHAKE

INGREDIENTS

- ❖ 1.5 cups whole frozen strawberries

- ❖ 1/2 cup frozen sliced banana

- ❖ 1/4 cup vanilla protein powder (any kind will work)

- ❖ 1/3 cup nonfat Greek yogurt

- ❖ 1 cup unsweetened almond milk

- ❖ Optional topping: crushed graham crackers

INSTRUCTIONS

1. Place all ingredients into a high-speed blender and blend until smooth. Add more almond milk as needed depending on preference.

3.HEALTHY CHOCOLATE PEANUT BUTTER SMOOTHIE

INGREDIENTS

- ❖ 2 cups sliced frozen bananas
- ❖ 3 tablespoons all-natural creamy peanut butter
- ❖ 1/4 cup cocoa powder
- ❖ 1 tablespoon ground flaxseed
- ❖ 1 cup packed spinach
- ❖ 1 cup almond milk

INSTRUCTIONS

1. Remove frozen bananas from the freezer and place them into a high-speed blender.

2. Next, add the rest of the ingredients to the blender and blend until smooth.

3. If the smoothie is too thick, slowly add a tablespoon of almond milk at a time until smoothie reaches desired consistency.

4.STRAWBERRY PINEAPPLE SMOOTHIE

INGREDIENTS

- ❖ cups frozen pineapple chunks

- ❖ 1.5 cups frozen strawberries

- ❖ 1/2 cup vanilla Greek yogurt

- ❖ 1 teaspoon vanilla extract

- ❖ 1.5 cups almond milk, unsweetened (or more to taste)

INSTRUCTIONS

1. Place all ingredients for your strawberry pineapple smoothie into a high-speed blender.

2. Blend on high until smooth. Depending on how frozen your fruit is, you may need to add more almond milk.

3. Serve with extra fresh pineapple chunks on the bottom.

5.STRAWBERRY BANANA SPINACH SMOOTHIE

INGREDIENTS

For the Meal Prep Smoothies Bags

- ❖ 2 cups frozen sliced bananas

- ❖ 2 cups frozen whole strawberries

- ❖ 4 cups fresh spinach

- ❖ 4 teaspoons chia seeds

For Serving (for 1 serving)

- ❖ 2 tablespoons vanilla protein powder (any kind)

- ❖ 1/2 cup unsweetened almond milk

INSTRUCTIONS

For the Bag

1. First, line a baking sheet with parchment paper. Then, evenly spread out 2 cups of sliced bananas, 2 cups of whole strawberries. Place in the freezer for about 2 hours or until completely frozen.

2. Next, take 4 quart-size freezer bags and write the date and Strawberry Banana Green Smoothie on the front. Add 1 cup of the frozen fruit, a handful of spinach, and a teaspoon of chia seeds to each bag.

3. Before sealing, make sure you squeeze as much

air out as possible to prevent freezer burn. Seal and place in the freezer for later use.

For Blending (for 1 serving)

4. Once you're ready to blend, empty contents of spinach smoothie bag into a high-speed blender.

5. Then, add about 1/2 cup of almond milk and 2 tablespoons of your favorite protein powder.

6. Blend on high for about 1 minute or until everything is blended.

6.LAYERED CHOCOLATE BANANA SMOOTHIE WITH PROTEIN

INGREDIENTS

For the Chocolate

- ❖ frozen bananas, medium
- ❖ 1/4 cup chocolate protein powder
- ❖ 1 tablespoon cocoa powder
- ❖ 1/3 cup vanilla Greek yogurt
- ❖ 1/2 cup vanilla unsweetened almond milk
- ❖ pinch of sea salt

For the Banana

- ❖ 1.5 frozen bananas, medium
- ❖ 1/4 cup vanilla protein powder
- ❖ 1 teaspoon vanilla extract
- ❖ 1/3 cup vanilla Greek yogurt
- ❖ 1/2 cup vanilla unsweetened almond milk

INSTRUCTIONS

For the Chocolate

1. Place all ingredients in a high-speed blender.

2. Then, turn to high and process for 60 seconds or until smooth.

For the Banana

3. Place all ingredients in a high-speed blender.

4. Then, turn to high and process for 60 seconds or until smooth.

7.TROPICAL SPINACH SMOOTHIE

INGREDIENTS

- ❖ 2 cups tropical blend frozen fruit

- ❖ 1/2 cup full fat canned coconut milk

- ❖ 1/2 cup water

- ❖ 2 cups packed fresh spinach

- ❖ 1 tablespoon ground flax seed

INSTRUCTIONS

1. Place all ingredients in a high-speed blender and mix until smooth.

8.REFRESHING GINGER PINEAPPLE SMOOTHIE

INGREDIENTS

- ❖ 1 cup frozen pineapple

- ❖ 1 teaspoon flax seed meal

- ❖ 1/2 medium banana, frozen

- ❖ 1/4 cup nonfat Greek yogurt, plain

- ❖ 2 teaspoons fresh ginger, grated (or more!!!)

- ❖ 1 cup 100% orange juice

INSTRUCTIONS

1. Place all ingredients into a blender. Blend until smooth and enjoy!

9. THE BEST GREEN SMOOTHIE RECIPES

INGREDIENTS

- ❖ 1 cup frozen fruit (banana, mixed berries, tropical mix)

- ❖ 1 cup of fresh greens (spinach, kale, or arugula)

- ❖ 1/2 – 1 cup milk (almond, soy, coconut, cows, etc.)

- ❖ 1/2 tablespoon ground seeds (flax, chia, etc.)

INSTRUCTIONS

1. Place all ingredients into a high-speed blender.

2. Blend on high until smooth. We recommend starting with 1/2 cup of milk and going up from there depending on how thick you like your smoothies.

3. Serve immediately.

10.SUPERFOOD PROTEIN SMOOTHIE

INGREDIENTS

- ❖ 1 cup frozen sliced bananas

- ❖ 1 cup frozen blueberries

- ❖ 1 cup fresh kale, packed

- ❖ 2 Medjool dates, pitted

- ❖ ½ tablespoon ground flaxseed

- ❖ 3 large frozen cauliflower florets

- ❖ ½ cup chocolate protein powder

- ❖ tablespoons cocoa powder

- ❖ 2 cups unsweetened almond milk* (or more to taste)

INSTRUCTIONS

1. Place all ingredients into a high-speed blender and blend until smooth.

11.PEANUT BUTTER BANANA COLD BREW PROTEIN SMOOTHIE

INGREDIENTS

- ❖ 1 large frozen banana

- ❖ 2 tablespoons all-natural peanut butter, creamy

- ❖ 1/4 cup vanilla protein powder (any kind)

- ❖ ¼ cup cold brew concentrate

- ❖ 1/2 cup unsweetened almond milk (or more, to taste)

INSTRUCTIONS

1. Place everything in the blender and blend until smooth

12. STRAWBERRY PINEAPPLE BANANA SMOOTHIE

INGREDIENTS

- ❖ 1 cup Strawberries
- ❖ 1/2 cup Pineapple
- ❖ 1 Banana
- ❖ 2 cups Orange Juice
- ❖ 1/2 cup Greek Yogurt
- ❖ 1 cup Spinach optional
- ❖ 1 Tablespoon Chia or Flaxseeds optional
- ❖ Ice

INSTRUCTIONS

1. Add ingredients into a blender and blend until smooth and creamy. Add ice depending on temperature preference.

2. Frozen bananas work best in smoothies. Peel, slice in half, and place in a large Ziploc bag in the freezer overnight.

3. Add more spinach and kale to increase nutritional benefits.

13.SWEET CHERRY ALMOND SMOOTHIE

INGREDIENTS

- ❖ 1 1/2 cups Cherries frozen
- ❖ 1 cup Almond Milk
- ❖ 1 scoop Protein Powder
- ❖ 1 Banana
- ❖ Ice
- ❖ Optional: top with unsweetened coconut flakes + almond butter

INSTRUCTIONS

1. Add ingredients into a blender and blend until smooth and creamy. Add ice depending on temperature preference.

2. Frozen bananas work best in smoothies. Peel, slice in half, and place in a large Ziploc bag in the freezer overnight.

3. Add more spinach and kale to increase nutritional benefits.

14.LOVELY GREENS SMOOTHIE

INGREDIENTS

- ❖ 1 cup Pineapple

- ❖ 2 cups Spinach

- ❖ 1/2 cup Grapes

- ❖ 1 1/2 cup Orange Juice

- ❖ 1 Banana

- ❖ Ice

INSTRUCTIONS

1. Add ingredients into a blender and blend until smooth and creamy. Add ice depending on temperature preference.

2. Frozen bananas work best in smoothies. Peel, slice in half, and place in a large Ziploc bag in the freezer overnight.

3. Add more spinach and kale to increase nutritional benefits.

15.CHOCOLATE POWERHOUSE SMOOTHIE:

INGREDIENTS

- ❖ 1 cup Coconut Milk
- ❖ 1 scoop Chocolate Protein Powder
- ❖ 1/2 cup Blueberries
- ❖ 1 cup Spinach
- ❖ 1 Banana
- ❖ 1 Tablespoon Almond Butter
- ❖ Ice

INSTRUCTIONS

1. Add ingredients into a blender and blend until smooth and creamy. Add ice depending on temperature preference.

2. Frozen bananas work best in smoothies. Peel, slice in half, and place in a large Ziploc bag in the freezer overnight.

3. Add more spinach and kale to increase nutritional benefits.

16.YOUTHFUL GLOW GREEN SMOOTHIE:

INGREDIENTS

- ❖ 2 Handfuls approximately 2 cups Kale or Power Greens Mix

- ❖ 2 Handfuls approximately 2 cups Baby Spinach

- ❖ 2 cups Pure Apple Juice

- ❖ 1/2 Cucumber

- ❖ 1/2 Lemon squeezed (for extra benefits, use the juice from an entire lemon)

- ❖ 1 Banana

- ❖ Ice

- ❖ Optional:

- ❖ 1 teaspoon Fresh Ginger grated

INSTRUCTIONS

1. Add ingredients into a blender and blend until smooth and creamy. Add ice depending on temperature preference.

2. Frozen bananas work best in smoothies. Peel, slice in half, and place in a large Ziploc bag in the freezer overnight.

3. Add more spinach and kale to increase nutritional benefits.

17.PEACHY MANGO SMOOTHIE

INGREDIENTS

- ❖ 1 cup Peaches
- ❖ 1 cup Mangoes
- ❖ 1 Banana
- ❖ 1 cup Orange Juice
- ❖ 1/4 teaspoon Turmeric
- ❖ 1/4 teaspoon Ginger

INSTRUCTIONS

1. Add ingredients into a blender and blend until smooth and creamy. Add ice depending on temperature preference.

2. Frozen bananas work best in smoothies. Peel, slice in half, and place in a large Ziploc bag in the freezer overnight.

3. Add more spinach and kale to increase nutritional benefits.

18.BEST PUMPKIN PANCAKES RECIPE

INGREDIENTS

- ❖ 1 c. all-purpose flour
- ❖ 1 c. whole wheat flour
- ❖ 1 tbsp. baking powder
- ❖ 1 tsp. pumpkin pie spice
- ❖ 1/2 tsp. baking soda
- ❖ 1/2 tsp. salt
- ❖ 1 c. whole milk
- ❖ 1/2 c. pumpkin purée
- ❖ 3 tbsp. brown sugar
- ❖ 2 large eggs
- ❖ 2 tbsp. vegetable oil
- ❖ whipped topping
- ❖ chocolate chips

DIRECTIONS

1. In large bowl, whisk all-purpose flour and whole wheat flour, baking powder, pumpkin pie spice, baking soda, and salt.

2. In small bowl, whisk whole milk, pumpkin purée, brown sugar, eggs, and vegetable oil; stir

into flour mixture until almost smooth.

3. Lightly grease 12-inch nonstick skillet; heat on medium until hot. In batches, scoop batter by 1/4-cupfuls batter into skillet, spreading to 3 1/2 inches each. Cook 2 to 3 minutes or until bubbly and edges are dry. Turn; cook 2 minutes or until golden.

4. Drizzle with syrup. Create "ghosts" with whipped topping; add chocolate chip "eyes."

19.BREAKFAST SUPER-SHAKE

INGREDIENTS

- ❖ 100ml full-fat milk
- ❖ 2 tbsp natural yogurt
- ❖ 1 banana
- ❖ 150g frozen fruits of the forest
- ❖ 50g blueberries
- ❖ 1 tbsp chia seeds
- ❖ ½ tsp cinnamon
- ❖ 1 tbsp goji berries
- ❖ 1 tsp mixed seeds
- ❖ 1 tsp honey (ideally Manuka)

INSTRUCTION

1. Put the ingredients in a blender and blitz until smooth. Pour into a glass and enjoy!

20.TWO-MINUTE BREAKFAST SMOOTHIE

INGREDIENTS

- ❖ 1 banana
- ❖ 1 tbsp porridge oats
- ❖ 80g soft fruit (whatever you have – strawberries, blueberries, and mango all work well)
- ❖ 150ml milk
- ❖ 1 tsp honey
- ❖ 1 tsp vanilla extract

INSTRUCTION

1. Put all the ingredients in a blender and whizz for 1 min until smooth.

2. Pour the banana oat smoothie into two glasses to serve.

21.STRAWBERRY GREEN GODDESS SMOOTHIE

INGREDIENTS

- ❖ 160g ripe strawberries, hulled
- ❖ 160g baby spinach
- ❖ 1 small avocado, halved and the flesh scooped out
- ❖ 150ml pot bio yogurt
- ❖ 2 small oranges, juiced, plus ½ tsp finely grated zest

INSTRUCTION

1. Put all the ingredients in a blender and whizz until completely smooth. If it's a little thick, add a drop of chilled water then blitz again. Pour into glasses and drink straight away.

22.STRAWBERRY SMOOTHIE

INGREDIENTS

- ❖ 10 strawberries, hulled (approx. 175g)
- ❖ 1 small banana, sliced
- ❖ 100ml orange juice, chilled

INSTRUCTION

1. Blitz the strawberries in a blender with the banana and orange juice until smooth.

2. Pour the smoothie into a tall glass to serve.

23.RASPBERRY AND APPLE SMOOTHIE

INGREDIENTS

- ❖ 2 apples, cored (we used Granny Smith)
- ❖ 150g frozen raspberries
- ❖ 150ml natural yogurt
- ❖ 2 tbsp porridge oats
- ❖ ½ lemon, juiced
- ❖ 100ml milk

INSTRUCTION

1. Tip all ingredients into a blender or smoothie maker and blitz until smooth, adding 50ml water or milk if it's too thick.

24.CARROT AND ORANGE SMOOTHIE

INGREDIENTS

- ❖ 2 medium carrots, peeled and roughly chopped or grated depending on your blender

- ❖ 2 oranges, peeled

- ❖ 2cm piece of ginger, grated

- ❖ 2 tbsp oats

- ❖ 100g ice

INSTRUCTION

1. Tip all the ingredients into a blender or smoothie maker and blitz until smooth, adding 150ml water if it's too thick – alter the consistency to your liking.

25.SUNSHINE SMOOTHIE

INGREDIENTS

- ❖ 500ml carrot juice, chilled
- ❖ 200g pineapple (fresh or canned)
- ❖ 2 bananas, broken into chunks
- ❖ small piece ginger, peeled
- ❖ 20g cashew nuts
- ❖ juice 1 lime

INSTRUCTION

1. Put the ingredients in a blender and whizz until smooth. Drink straight away or pour into a bottle to drink on the go. Will keep in the fridge for a day.

26.BANANA SMOOTHIE

INGREDIENTS

- ❖ 500ml unsweetened almond milk
- ❖ 2 tbsp almond butter
- ❖ 6 prunes
- ❖ 1 tsp cinnamon
- ❖ 1 small ripe banana

INSTRUCTION

1. In a blender, whizz the almond milk with the almond butter, prunes, cinnamon and banana.

2. Transfer to 2 bottles and chill until ready to drink, or pack for lunch on the go. The smoothies will keep in the fridge for 2 days.

28.MANGO LASSI

INGREDIENTS

- ❖ 3-4 ripe mangoes (honey mangoes if possible)
- ❖ 500g natural yogurt
- ❖ a pinch ground cardamom (crush the seeds from 1-2 pods)
- ❖ 1 tbsp honey
- ❖ 2 limes, juiced, to taste

INSTRUCTION

1. Put all the ingredients apart from the lime juice in a food processor and blitz. Add the lime juice along with a pinch of salt, to taste, if the cardamom isn't strong enough then add a little more, then pour into glasses with some ice cubes and serve

29.KALE SMOOTHIE

INGREDIENTS

- ❖ 2 handfuls kale
- ❖ ½ avocado
- ❖ ½ lime, juice only
- ❖ large handful frozen pineapple chunks
- ❖ medium-sized chunk ginger
- ❖ 1 tbsp cashew nuts
- ❖ 1 banana, optional

INSTRUCTION

1. Put all of the ingredients into a bullet or smoothie maker, add a large splash of water and blitz. Add more water until you have the desired consistency.

30.CHERRY SMOOTHIE

INGREDIENTS

- ❖ 300g frozen or fresh cherries, pitted
- ❖ 150g natural yogurt
- ❖ 1 large banana, sliced
- ❖ ½ tsp vanilla extract

INSTRUCTION

1. Tip all the ingredients into a blender and blitz until smooth. Adjust the thickness to your liking with 50-100ml cold water. Serve in four glasses or chill for up to 24 hrs, giving a good stir before serving.

31.COCONUT & BANANA SMOOTHIE

INGREDIENTS

- ❖ 100g coconut yogurt

- ❖ 3 tbsp milk of your choice (we used unsweetened almond milk)

- ❖ ½ tsp ground turmeric

- ❖ 3cm piece of fresh ginger, peeled

- ❖ 2 tsp baobab powder (optional)

- ❖ 1 small ripe banana

- ❖ 1 tsp honey

- ❖ 1 tbsp oats

- ❖ juice of 0.5 a lemon

INSTRUCTION

1. Add the coconut yogurt and milk to a high-speed blender then add the turmeric, fresh ginger and baobab powder (if using). Tip in the remaining ingredients then blend until smooth. Add ice and blitz again if you prefer a colder drink. Pour into glasses and serve.

32.TURMERIC SMOOTHIE BOWL

INGREDIENTS

- ❖ 10cm/4in fresh turmeric, or 2 tsp ground turmeric

- ❖ 3 tbsp coconut milk yogurt (we used Co Yoh), or the cream skimmed from the top of canned coconut milk

- ❖ 50g gluten-free oats

- ❖ 1 tbsp cashew butter (or a handful of cashews)

- ❖ 2 bananas, peeled and roughly chopped

- ❖ ½ tsp ground cinnamon

- ❖ 1 tbsp chia seeds or chopped nuts, to serve

INSTRUCTION

1. Peel the turmeric root, if using, and grate. Put all ingredients in a blender with 600ml water and blend until smooth. Serve in a bowl with chia seeds or some chopped nuts sprinkled over.

33.KEFIR BREAKFAST SMOOTHIE

INGREDIENTS

- ❖ 1 large mango, stoned and chopped
- ❖ 2cm piece ginger, finely grated
- ❖ ½ tsp ground turmeric
- ❖ 200ml fresh orange juice
- ❖ 300ml kefir
- ❖ 1-2 tbsp honey or agave, to taste

INSTRUCTION

1. Put all the ingredients in a blender and blitz until completely smooth. Taste and add a little more ginger, turmeric and honey, if you like.

2. Pour into two tall glasses and serve. Can be chilled in a covered jug in the fridge for up to 24 hrs.

34.VEGAN SMOOTHIE

INGREDIENTS

- ❖ 100ml (¼ tall glass) cherry juice (we used Cherry good)

- ❖ 200ml (½ tall glass) unsweetened soya milk

- ❖ 1 cherry soya yogurt

- ❖ 3 tbsp or 50g firm silken tofu

- ❖ 75g (1 empty yogurt pot) frozen cherry

- ❖ 2 tbsp porridge oat

INSTRUCTION

1. Measure all the ingredients exactly or use a tall glass and your empty yogurt pot for speed – they don't have to be exact. Put them into a blender and blitz until smooth. Pour into 1 tall glass (you'll have enough for a top up) or two short tumblers.

35.CREAMY MANGO & COCONUT SMOOTHIE

INGREDIENTS

- ❖ 200ml (½ tall glass) coconut milk (we used Kara Dairy Free)

- ❖ 4 tbsp coconut milk yogurt (we used Coyo)

- ❖ 1 banana

- ❖ 1 tbsp ground flaxseed, sunflower and pumpkin seed (we used Linwood's)

- ❖ 120g (¼ bag) frozen mango chunks

- ❖ 1 passion fruit, to finish (optional)

INSTRUCTION

1. Measure all the ingredients or use a tall glass for speed – they don't have to be exact. Put them into a blender and blitz until smooth. Pour into 1 tall glass (you'll have enough for a top up) or two short tumblers. Cut the passion fruit in half, if using, and scrape the seeds on top.

36.PEACH MELBA SMOOTHIE

INGREDIENTS

- ❖ 410g can peach halves
- ❖ 100g frozen raspberry, plus a few for garnish
- ❖ 100ml orange juice
- ❖ 150ml fresh custard, plus a spoonful for garnish

INSTRUCTION

1. Drain and rinse peaches and place in a blender with raspberries. Add orange juice and fresh custard and whizz together.

2. Pour over ice, garnish with another spoonful of custard and a few raspberries. Best served chilled.

37.SUPER BERRY SMOOTHIE

INGREDIENTS

- ❖ 450g bag frozen berry
- ❖ 450g pot fat-free strawberry yogurt
- ❖ 100ml milk
- ❖ 25g porridge oat
- ❖ 2 tsp honey (optional)

INSTRUCTION

1. Whizz the berries, yogurt and milk together with a stick blender until smooth. Stir through the porridge oats, then pour into 4 glasses and serve with a drizzle of honey, if you like.

38.CRANBERRY & RASPBERRY SMOOTHIE

INGREDIENTS

- ❖ 200ml cranberry juice

- ❖ 175g frozen raspberry, defrosted

- ❖ 100ml milk

- ❖ 200ml natural yogurt

- ❖ 1 tbsp caster sugar, or to taste

- ❖ mint sprigs, to serve

INSTRUCTION

1. Place all the ingredients into a blender and pulse until smooth. Pour into glasses and serve topped with fresh mint.

39.MANGO & BANANA SMOOTHIE

INGREDIENTS

- ❖ 1 medium mango
- ❖ 1 banana
- ❖ 500ml orange juice
- ❖ 4 ice cubes

INSTRUCTION

1. Cut the mango down either side of the flat stone, then peel and cut the flesh into chunks.

2. Peel and chop the banana.

3. Put all the ingredients into a food processor or blender, then process until smooth and thick. Keep in the fridge and use the day you make it.

40.STRAWBERRY BREAKFAST SMOOTHIE

INGREDIENTS

- ❖ 1 small ripe banana

- ❖ about 140g blackberries, blueberries, raspberries or strawberries (or use a mix), plus extra to serve

- ❖ apple juice or mineral water, optional

- ❖ runny honey, to serve

INSTRUCTION

1. Slice the banana into your blender or food processor and add the berries of your choice. Whizz until smooth. With the blades whirring, pour in juice or water to make the consistency you like. Toss a few extra fruits on top, drizzle with honey and serve.

41.TROPICAL BREAKFAST SMOOTHIE

INGREDIENTS

- ❖ 3 passion fruits
- ❖ 1 banana, chopped
- ❖ 1small mango, peeled, stoned and chopped
- ❖ 300ml orange juice
- ❖ ice cubes

INSTRUCTION

1. Scoop the pulp of the passion fruits into a blender and add the banana, mango and orange juice. Purée until smooth and drink immediately, topped with ice cubes.

42.BANANA, CLEMENTINE & MANGO SMOOTHIE

INGREDIENTS

- ❖ about 24 juicy clementine, plus an extra one for decoration

- ❖ 2 small, very ripe and juicy mangoes

- ❖ 2 ripe bananas

- ❖ 500g tub whole milk or low-fat yogurt

- ❖ handful of ice cubes (optional)

INSTRUCTION

1. Halve the clementine and squeeze out the juice – you should have about 600ml/1 pint. (This can be done the night before.) Peel the mangoes, slice the fruit away from the stone in the center, then chop the flesh into rough pieces. Peel and slice the bananas.

2. Put the clementine juice, mango flesh, bananas, yogurt and ice cubes into a liquidizer and blend until smooth. Pour into six glasses and serve. (You might need to make this in two batches, depending on the size of your liquidizer.) If you don't add ice cubes, chill in the fridge until ready to serve.

43.FOREST FRUIT & BANANA SMOOTHIE

INGREDIENTS

- ❖ frozen fruits of the forest

- ❖ banana, sliced

- ❖ low-fat fruits of the forest yogurt

INSTRUCTION

1. Whizz frozen fruits of the forest and sliced banana in a food processor with low-fat fruits of the forest yogurt.

44.SMOOTHIE JELLIES WITH ICE CREAM

INGREDIENTS

- ❖ 6 sheets leaf gelatin

- ❖ 1l bottle orange, mango and passion fruit smoothie (we used Innocent)

- ❖ To serve

- ❖ 500ml tub good-quality vanilla ice cream such as Green & Black's (you might not need it all)

INSTRUCTION

1. Put the leaf gelatin into a bowl and cover with cold water. Leave for a few mins until soft and floppy. Meanwhile, gently heat the smoothie in a saucepan without boiling. Take off the heat. Lift the gelatin out of the water, squeeze out the excess water, then add it to the smoothie pan. Stir well until smooth, then pour into 12 moulds, pots or glasses, or use 24 shot-glass-sized pots. Chill for at least 1 hr to set.

2. For perfect mini scoops of ice cream, dip a tbsp measuring spoon into a cup of hot water, then shake off the excess. Scoop the ice cream, dipping the spoon in the hot water each time. Serve each smoothie jelly topped with ice cream.

45.SMOOTHIE CUBES

INGREDIENTS

- ❖ Blackberries
- ❖ Strawberries
- ❖ Raspberries
- ❖ passion fruit
- ❖ mango
- ❖ any other fruits you like

INSTRUCTION

1. Purée a fruit (try blackberries, strawberries, raspberries, passion fruit and mango, in a food processor, leave pips in or sieve.

2. Freeze in ice trays ready to whizz up (3 per serving) with a banana, 150ml pot plain yogurt, and milk and honey to taste.

46.GREEN GODDESS SMOOTHIE BOWL

INGREDIENTS

- ❖ 2 bananas, sliced

- ❖ 1 ripe avocado, stoned, peeled and chopped into chunks

- ❖ 1 small ripe mango, stoned, peeled and chopped into chunks

- ❖ 100g spinach (fresh or frozen)

- ❖ 250ml milk (unsweetened almond or coconut milk works well)

- ❖ 1 tbsp unsweetened almond or peanut butter

- ❖ 1 tbsp clear honey, agave or maple syrup (optional)

For the seed mix

- ❖ 1 tbsp chia seeds

- ❖ 1 tbsp linseeds

- ❖ 4 tbsp pumpkin seeds

- ❖ 4 tbsp sunflower seeds

- ❖ 4 tbsp coconut flakes

- ❖ 4 tbsp flaked almonds

- ❖ ¼ tsp ground cinnamon

- ❖ 2 tbsp clear honey, agave or maple syrup

To serve

- ❖ 175g mixed fresh fruit, chopped (we used banana, mango, raspberries and blueberries)

INSTRUCTION

1. Slice the bananas and arrange over a small baking tray lined with parchment. Freeze for 2 hrs until solid. (You can now transfer the banana slices to a freezer bag and freeze for 3 months, or continue with the recipe.)

2. For the seed mix, heat oven to 180C/160C fan/gas 4 and line a baking tray with parchment. Tip the seeds, coconut and almonds into a bowl, add the cinnamon and drizzle over the honey, agave or maple syrup. Toss until everything is well coated, then scatter over the baking tray in an even layer. Bake for 10-15 mins, stirring every 5 mins or so, until the seeds are lightly toasted. Leave to cool. Will keep in an airtight container for up to 1 month.

3. Put the avocado, mango, spinach, milk, nut butter, frozen banana slices and honey (if using) in a blender and whizz to a thick smoothie consistency – you may have to scrape down the sides with a spoon a few times. Divide between two bowls and arrange the fruit on top. Scatter 1-2 tbsp of the seed mix over each bowl and eat straight away.

47.VITAMIN BOOSTER SMOOTHIE

INGREDIENTS

- ❖ 1 orange, peeled and roughly chopped
- ❖ 1 large carrot, peeled and roughly chopped
- ❖ 2 sticks celery, roughly chopped
- ❖ 50g mango, roughly chopped
- ❖ 200ml water

INSTRUCTION

1. Put all the orange, carrot, celery and mango in the blender, top up with water, then blitz until smooth.

48.AVOCADO SMOOTHIE

INGREDIENTS

- ❖ ½ avocado, peeled, stoned and roughly chopped
- ❖ generous handful spinach
- ❖ generous handful kale, washed well
- ❖ 50g pineapple chunks
- ❖ 10cm piece cucumber, roughly chopped
- ❖ 300ml coconut water

INSTRUCTION

1. Put the avocado, spinach, kale, pineapple and cucumber in the blender.

2. Top up with coconut water, then blitz until smooth.

49.HEART HELPER SMOOTHIE

INGREDIENTS

- ❖ 2 small raw beetroots, peeled and roughly chopped

- ❖ 1 small apple peeled, quartered and cored

- ❖ 50g blueberry

- ❖ 1 tbsp grated ginger

- ❖ 300ml water

INSTRUCTION

1. Put the beetroot, apple, blueberries and ginger in a blender, top up with water then blitz until smooth.

50.AVOCADO & STRAWBERRY SMOOTHIE

INGREDIENTS

- ❖ ½ avocado, stoned, peeled and cut into chunks
- ❖ 150g strawberry, halved
- ❖ 4 tbsp low-fat natural yogurt
- ❖ 200ml semi-skimmed milk
- ❖ lemon or lime juice, to taste
- ❖ honey, to taste

INSTRUCTION

1. Put all the ingredients in a blender and whizz until smooth. If the consistency is too thick, add a little water.

CONCLUSION

Whether you're looking for a way to add some nutrition to your daily diet or seeking to learn more about smoothies to begin your first cleanse, you now have some excellent recipes and tips to get you started. Remember, though, to use this as a general guide. Once you get the hang of mixing flavors, feel free to make up your own blends to suit your tastes and health goals.

The Super Healthy Smoothie recipes

50 Essential Smoothies to Get Healthy

Donnie King

All rights reserved.

Disclaimer

The information contained i is meant to serve as a comprehensive collection of strategies that the author of this eBook has done research about. Summaries, strategies, tips and tricks are only recommendation by the author, and reading this eBook will not guarantee that one's results will exactly mirror the author's results. The author of the eBook has made all reasonable effort to provide current and accurate information for the readers of the eBook. The author and it's associates will not be held liable for any unintentional error or omissions that may be found. The material in the eBook may include information by third parties. Third party materials comprise of opinions expressed by their owners. As such, the author of the eBook does not assume responsibility or liability for any third party material or opinions. Whether because of the progression of the internet, or the unforeseen changes in company policy and editorial submission guidelines, what is stated as fact at the time of this writing may become outdated or inapplicable later.

The eBook is copyright © 2021 with all rights reserved. It is illegal to redistribute, copy, or create derivative work from this eBook whole or in part. No parts of this report may be reproduced or retransmitted in any reproduced or retransmitted in any forms whatsoever without the writing expressed and signed permission from the author.

INTRODUCTION

A smoothie recipe is a drink made from pureed raw fruit and/or vegetables, using a blender. A smoothie often has a liquid base such as water, fruit juice, dairy products, such as milk, yogurt, ice cream or cottage cheese.

1.TAHINI DATE AND CINNAMON SMOOTHIE

INGREDIENTS

- ❖ 1/2–1 frozen banana (depending on sweetness)
- ❖ 3/4 cup milk of choice (we like vanilla almond milk)
- ❖ 1 Medjool date, pitted
- ❖ 1 tbsp cinnamon
- ❖ 2 tbsp tahini
- ❖ Pinch of salt
- ❖ Optional: frozen spinach, flaxseed, protein powder

INSTRUCTIONS

1. Place all ingredients in a blender and blend on high until smooth.

2.SWEET POTATO SMOOTHIE BOWL [TASTES LIKE SWEET POTATO PIE!]

INGREDIENTS

- ❖ 1 small sweet potato
- ❖ 1/2 cup steamed then frozen zucchini*
- ❖ 1 small banana, frozen
- ❖ 1/3 cup yogurt (+ more for topping) or use dairy-free yogurt
- ❖ 1/2 cup unsweetened vanilla almond milk (more for a thinner consistency)
- ❖ 1 tsp pumpkin pie spice
- ❖ 1/4 tsp cardamom
- ❖ fresh ginger (about the size of your fingernail)

INSTRUCTIONS

1. To cook the sweet potato:
2. slice the sweet potato in half and then steam in a steamer basket for 10 mins
3. OR wrap in foil and place in a 350-degree oven for 1 hour.
4. See instructions above for microwave.
5. For smoothie:
6. Place all ingredients into a blender and blend until smooth.
7. Top with additional yogurt and pumpkin spice or toppings of choice

3.MATCHA MINT COCONUT SMOOTHIE BOWL

INGREDIENTS

- ❖ 1 large banana
- ❖ 1 tsp matcha powder
- ❖ 1/4–1/2 cup coconut milk*
- ❖ 3 fresh mint leaves
- ❖ 1 handful of baby spinach
- ❖ 3–4 ice cubes
- ❖ optional: 1/4 tsp cinnamon
- ❖ toppings: fresh fruit, yogurt (can use coconut yogurt), granola, etc....

INSTRUCTIONS

1. Add all ingredients (except toppings) to a high-speed blender.
2. Blend until well-combined
3. Pour into a bowl and top with toppings.
4. Eat immediately

The less you use, the thicker it will be, but it will also be more challenging to blend. Start with a 1/4 cup and add more if you need to get things moving.

4.YOGA GLOW SMOOTHIE + MY NEW MORNING ROUTINE

INGREDIENTS

- ❖ 1 cup blueberries
- ❖ 1/2 ripe banana
- ❖ 1/2 avocado
- ❖ 1–2 cups kale
- ❖ 1 knob fresh ginger, peeled and chopped
- ❖ 1/4 tsp turmeric
- ❖ 1 tbsp raw cacao
- ❖ 1/2 tsp maca powder
- ❖ 1/2 tsp cinnamon
- ❖ pinch of sea salt
- ❖ 1 cup Simple Truth Vapor Distilled Water (I use the blueberry-blackberry flavored)
- ❖ optional: a scoop of protein powder.

INSTRUCTIONS

1. Place all ingredients in a blender and blend until smooth.

5.ALMOND CHAI GREEN SMOOTHIE

INGREDIENTS

- ❖ 1 frozen banana
- ❖ 1 scoop vanilla protein powder of choice (I used Vega Sport Protein)
- ❖ 1/2 tsp ground ginger
- ❖ 1/4 tsp ground cinnamon
- ❖ 1/4 tsp ground cardamom
- ❖ 1/8 tsp ground nutmeg
- ❖ 1 scoop natural, smooth almond butter
- ❖ 2 cups baby spinach
- ❖ 1 cup unsweetened almond milk
- ❖ optional: 1/2 tsp vanilla extract

INSTRUCTIONS

1. Add ingredients to a blender in the order listed.
2. Blend until smooth.
3. Serve with toppings of choice. I like hemp seeds, added cinnamon, and almond butter.

6.BLUEBERRY GREEN SMOOTHIE BOWL

INGREDIENTS
- ❖ 1 cup frozen blueberries
- ❖ 1 scoop vanilla plant-based protein powder (I used Vega + Greens)
- ❖ 1/2 large banana (fresh or frozen)
- ❖ 1/4–1/2 cup almond milk (start with 1/4 cup and add more if your blender needs it)
- ❖ 1/4 avocado
- ❖ 2 cups greens (I use spinach, arugula, and kale)
- ❖ Some topping suggestions: Almond/Peanut Butter, granola, chia seeds, hemp seeds, pumpkin seeds, etc....

INSTRUCTIONS
1. Place all ingredients into a high-speed blender and blend on high until well-combined. If you prefer an even thicker smoothie, add in a couple of ice cubes.
2. Top with desired toppings and serve in a bowl.

7.PINEAPPLE MOJITO GREEN SMOOTHIE

INGREDIENTS

- ❖ 1/2 cup coconut milk (I used carton) or other non-dairy milk
- ❖ 1/4 cup fresh mint
- ❖ 1 1/2 cups chopped pineapple (fresh or frozen)
- ❖ 1–2 cups baby spinach
- ❖ 1 lime, zest, and juice
- ❖ 1/2 tsp freshly grated ginger
- ❖ 1 cup ice
- ❖ Optional: Top with chia seeds, shredded coconut, hemp seeds, etc....

INSTRUCTIONS

1. Add all ingredients to a high-powered blender until well-combined.
2. Top with desired toppings.

8.MANGO ALMOND BUTTER SMOOTHIE

INGREDIENTS

- ❖ 1 cup frozen mango
- ❖ 1/2 frozen banana, sliced
- ❖ 1/2 cup almond milk*
- ❖ 1 tbsp almond butter
- ❖ 1 scoop vanilla protein powder
- ❖ optional: 2 cups spinach for an extra veggie boost.

INSTRUCTIONS

1. Join all fixings in your blender.
2. Drink right away.

This smoothie is thick, so if you like to drink with a straw instead of eating with a spoon, add a touch more almond milk.

9.CARROT CAKE SMOOTHIE BOWL

INGREDIENTS

- ❖ 1 cup chopped romaine (I didn't have romaine, so I used spinach)
- ❖ 1 cup unsweetened coconut milk
- ❖ 2 cups chopped raw carrots
- ❖ 1 cup chopped pineapple
- ❖ 1 banana
- ❖ 2 clementine, peeled (also didn't have so I used mango)
- ❖ 1/2 teaspoon vanilla extract
- ❖ dash of ground cinnamon and nutmeg

INSTRUCTIONS

1. Blend the romaine (or spinach) and coconut milk until smooth.
2. Add the remaining ingredients and blend again until smooth.
3. Top with pistachios and toasted coconut!

10.HOLIDAY DETOX GREEN APPLE SMOOTHIE

INGREDIENTS

- ❖ 1 banana (or half is plenty if you're watching sugar)
- ❖ 1–2 cups kale, stems removed
- ❖ 1 cup apple cider (no sugar added – just the real stuff)
- ❖ 1 cup water or ice
- ❖ optional extras: flax meal, nuts (I used pecans), nut butter
- ❖ dash of cinnamon
- ❖ pomegranate seeds for topping

INSTRUCTIONS

1. Mix all fixings until smooth. Use water for a juice-like surface and ice for a smoothie-like character. Include any additional items you need for extra protein, fiber, or solid fats.
2. Mix in a scramble of cinnamon, top with pomegranate seeds, and appreciate!

11.HONEY AND WILD BLUEBERRY SMOOTHIE

INGREDIENTS

- ❖ 1 banana, fresh or frozen
- ❖ 1 cup mango chunks, fresh or frozen
- ❖ 1/2 cup wild blueberries, fresh or frozen
- ❖ 1/2 cup plain non-fat Greek yogurt
- ❖ 1/2 cup milk (or just enough to help things blend smoothly)
- ❖ 1 heaping tablespoon raw honey (more to taste)
- ❖ 1/2 cup kale or any other add-ins that you want

INSTRUCTIONS

1. Place bananas, mangoes, blueberries, yogurt, and milk in a blender. Blend until smooth. Add the kale and honey; blend again until smooth.
2. If desired (and especially if all your ingredients were fresh instead of frozen), add a few ice cubes to increase the smoothie's volume and help it stay chilled. Crush until smooth.

12.BERRY GREEN SMOOTHIE

INGREDIENTS

- ❖ 3 small bananas
- ❖ 1/2 cup milk
- ❖ 1–2 handfuls of spinach
- ❖ 1 cup frozen berries (blueberries, blackberries, etc.)
- ❖ 1/2 cup bran cereal such as All-Bran original
- ❖ 1–2 tablespoons sweetener (sugar, honey, Trivia, agave, etc.)
- ❖ ice cubes (optional)

INSTRUCTIONS

1. Mix bananas and milk until smooth. Add spinach and mix on a high setting until the spinach's vast majority has been separated into tiny pieces. Add the frozen berries and mix until the smoothie combination is every one of the one tones.
2. Add the wheat and sugar; mix until wanted consistency. Add ice 3D shapes and mix again until smooth (discretionary – I generally don't).
3. Top with additional blueberries and serve immediately.

13.SIMPLE COCONUT GREEN SMOOTHIE

INGREDIENTS

- ❖ 1 cup Bai5 Antioxidant Infusions Molokai Coconut
- ❖ 1 heaping cup frozen peaches
- ❖ 1 cup spinach
- ❖ 2 tablespoons flax meal

INSTRUCTIONS

1. Defrost the peaches, so they are as yet frozen, yet delicate. I typically put them in the microwave for 30 seconds to one moment, or I forget about them on the counter for 15-20 minutes. This will help the surface of the smoothie.
2. Mix the Bai5 Molokai Coconut, frozen peaches, spinach, and flax supper for 2-3 minutes or until smooth. Taste and change by your loving. Serve or refrigerate right away.

14. WORLD'S BEST WATERMELON SMOOTHIE

INGREDIENTS

- ❖ 2 cups frozen cubed watermelon
- ❖ 1 cup water
- ❖ 1 tablespoon of honey or other sweeteners to taste
- ❖ a few mint and basil leaves, if you want to take it to the next level

INSTRUCTIONS

1. Blend the watermelon and the water until smooth. Add the honey and mint and blend for another 10-20 seconds until a mostly soft and slushy consistency.
2. Serve immediately!

15.MANGO SMOOTHIE RECIPE

INGREDIENTS

- ❖ 1 ½ cups frozen mango chunks
- ❖ 1 tablespoon chia seeds (optional)
- ❖ 1 ½ cups liquid (coconut water, almond milk, dairy milk, water)

INSTRUCTIONS

1. Combine all ingredients in a blender and blend until smooth. If the blender gets stuck, add in more liquid until it blends again.

16.GOJI PEACH CHERRY SMOOTHIE

INGREDIENTS

- ❖ 1 cup frozen cherries
- ❖ ½ cup frozen peach slices
- ❖ 1 ¼ cup almond milk
- ❖ 1 tablespoon goji berries
- ❖ Optional
- ❖ 1 tablespoon chia seeds
- ❖ 1 teaspoon ground flax
- ❖ 1-2 handfuls of spinach

INSTRUCTIONS

1. Place everything in the base of a blender and blend until smooth.

17.CHAI-SPICED STRAWBERRY MANGO SMOOTHIE

INGREDIENTS

- ❖ ¾ cup mango chunks (frozen)
- ❖ ¾ cup strawberries (frozen)
- ❖ 1 ¼ cups almond milk (or more as needed to blend; swap for dairy milk or your favorite blending liquid)
- ❖ ⅛ teaspoon chai spice blend (see notes *)
- ❖ ¼ teaspoon vanilla extract
- ❖ Optional
- ❖ 1 tablespoon chia seeds
- ❖ 1 teaspoon ground flax
- ❖ 1 cup spinach

INSTRUCTIONS

1. Place all ingredients in a blender and blend until smooth

18.BLUEBERRY COCONUT WATER SMOOTHIE

INGREDIENTS

- ❖ 1 ½ cups frozen blueberries
- ❖ 1 cup coconut water
- ❖ ½ cup yogurt full-fat plain or Greek
- ❖ ¼ teaspoon coconut extract
- ❖ 1 tablespoon hemp hearts

INSTRUCTIONS

1. Combine all ingredients in the blender and blend until smooth.

19.ANTI-INFLAMMATORY TURMERIC SMOOTHIE

INGREDIENTS

- ❖ 1 ¼ cups almond milk
- ❖ 1 cup kale or spinach packed
- ❖ ¼ teaspoon turmeric
- ❖ 1 pinch black pepper
- ❖ 1 tablespoon chia seeds
- ❖ 1 ½ cups pineapple chunks frozen

INSTRUCTIONS

1. Combine the first 5 ingredients in a blender and blend until smooth.
2. Add the pineapple chunks and blend again until completely smooth.

20.KETO GREEN SMOOTHIE

INGREDIENTS

- ❖ 1 cup cold water
- ❖ 1 cup baby spinach
- ❖ 1/2 cup cilantro
- ❖ 1-inch ginger - peeled
- ❖ 3/4 English cucumber - peeled
- ❖ 1/2-1 lemon - peeled
- ❖ 1 cup frozen avocado

INSTRUCTIONS

1. Add all ingredients to a high-speed blender and blend until smooth.
2. Store in an air-tight container such as a mason jar in the fridge for up to 3 days.

21.CHOCOLATE PEANUT BUTTER BANANA SMOOTHIE

INGREDIENTS

- ❖ 1 frozen banana
- ❖ 1 cup coconut milk frozen in the ice cube tray
- ❖ 3 Tbsp raw cacao powder
- ❖ 2 Tbsp hemp seeds
- ❖ 1 Tbsp peanut butter
- ❖ 1/2-1 cup almond milk
- ❖ 1 Tbsp maple syrup - (optional)

INSTRUCTIONS

1. Add all ingredients to a blender. Start with adding only 1/2 cup almond milk and add more if your blender needs the extra liquid or you like your smoothie more liquid.
2. Serve and enjoy!

22.BLUE SMOOTHIE

INGREDIENTS

- ❖ 2 frozen bananas
- ❖ 3 Tbsp hemp seeds
- ❖ 1 cup almond milk - (or coconut milk or any other milk of choice)
- ❖ 1-3 tsp Butterfly Pea Tea Powder - (depending on how blue you want your smoothie)

INSTRUCTIONS

1. Add all ingredients to a high-speed blender and then serve.

23.DRAGON FRUIT SMOOTHIE

INGREDIENTS
- ❖ 3/4 cup light coconut milk
- ❖ 1 dragon fruit
- ❖ 1 cup blackberries

INSTRUCTIONS
1. The night before, put coconut milk in an ice cube tray and freeze until solid.
2. Peel dragon fruit with a knife or by hand (as shown in the video).
3. Add dragon fruit, frozen coconut milk cubes, and blackberries to a high-speed blender and blend until smooth.
4. Serve and enjoy immediately.

24.AVOCADO SPINACH SMOOTHIE

INGREDIENTS

- ❖ 1 cup diced frozen mango
- ❖ 1/2 avocado
- ❖ 2 hands full baby spinach
- ❖ 2-3 Tbsp protein powder
- ❖ 1 cup cold water

INSTRUCTIONS

1. Add all ingredients to your blender. Blend until smooth. Enjoy immediately.

25.BANANA SMOOTHIE

INGREDIENTS

- ❖ 1/2 cup ice cubes
- ❖ large Bananas cut into chunks (frozen or fresh)
- ❖ 1/4 pineapple cubed (frozen or fresh)
- ❖ 1 cup pineapple juice or apple juice

INSTRUCTIONS

1. Blend all ingredients until smooth. Enjoy cold!

26.STRAWBERRY BLUEBERRY SMOOTHIE

INGREDIENTS

- ❖ 1/2 cup skim milk
- ❖ 1/2 cup blueberries fresh or frozen
- ❖ 1 cup strawberries fresh or frozen
- ❖ 6 ounces non-fat vanilla yogurt

INSTRUCTIONS

1. Add milk, blueberries, strawberries, and yogurt to a blender. Blend until smooth! If you are utilizing a new natural product, you may have to add ice to thicken. Appreciate cold.

27.PEACH SMOOTHIE

INGREDIENTS

- ❖ 1 medium banana cut in chunks
- ❖ 1 ripe peach pitted and sliced
- ❖ 1 (6) oz low-fat peach yogurt
- ❖ 1/4 cup orange juice
- ❖ 1 cup small ice cubes

INSTRUCTIONS

1. Combine all ingredients in a blender container; blend 1 to 2 minutes or until smooth and frothy.

28.WATERMELON SMOOTHIE

INGREDIENTS

- ❖ 1 1/2 cups watermelon cubed
- ❖ 1 cup strawberries trimmed
- ❖ 1/2 cup milk
- ❖ 1 tsp lemon juice
- ❖ 2 SPLENDA Naturals Stevia Sweetener packets
- ❖ 1/2 cup ice

INSTRUCTIONS

1. Add all ingredients to a blender and blend until combined. Serve cold.

29.BLUEBERRY SMOOTHIE

INGREDIENTS

- ❖ 1 Frozen banana thawed for 10-15 minutes
- ❖ 1/2 cup Skim Milk
- ❖ 1 cup Fat-Free Vanilla Yogurt
- ❖ 1 1/2 tsp Flax Seed Meal
- ❖ 2/3 cup Frozen Blueberries

INSTRUCTIONS

1. Cut your banana into small pieces. Add bananas, milk, yogurt, and a flaxseed meal to a blender. Beat 5-10 seconds until smooth. Gradually add the blueberries while blending on low. Increase speed, and blend till you've reached your desired consistency.

30.STRAWBERRY OATMEAL SMOOTHIE

INGREDIENTS

- ❖ 1 cup skim milk
- ❖ 1/2 cup rolled oats
- ❖ 1 banana broken into chunks
- ❖ 1 cup frozen strawberries
- ❖ 1/2 tsp vanilla extract
- ❖ 1 tsp white sugar

INSTRUCTIONS

1. Use a blender to grind up oats.
2. Add milk, oats, bananas and strawberries; blend well.
3. Add vanilla and sugar if desired. Blend until smooth.
4. Serve cold

31.PEACH RASPBERRY SMOOTHIE

INGREDIENTS

- ❖ 1 cup sliced peaches
- ❖ 1/2 cup frozen raspberries
- ❖ 1 cup vanilla unsweetened almond milk or milk of your choice
- ❖ 1-2 teaspoons agave or honey depending on the sweetness of your peaches
- ❖ 3-4 ice cubes

INSTRUCTIONS

1. Add peaches and raspberries to the blender
2. Add milk, agave or honey, and ice cubes to the blender.
3. Blend until smooth. Serve immediately.

32.SECRET INGREDIENT HEALTHY SMOOTHIE

INGREDIENTS

- ❖ 1 1/4 cups unsweetened vanilla almond milk (or milk of choice or kefir)
- ❖ 1 banana peeled (fresh or frozen)
- ❖ 1 cup frozen blueberries
- ❖ 1/2 cup frozen cauliflower florets
- ❖ 1 cup packed spinach leaves
- ❖ 1 teaspoon chia seeds
- ❖ 1 teaspoon ground flaxseed
- ❖ 1 scoop vanilla protein powder optional

INSTRUCTIONS

1. Place the milk, banana, blueberries, cauliflower, spinach, chia seeds, ground flaxseed, and protein powder, if using, in a blender. Blend until smooth. If the smoothie is too thick, you can add a little more milk or water and blend again until desired consistency is reached. Pour into a glass or two glasses and serve immediately.

33.BLACKBERRY LIME SMOOTHIE

INGREDIENTS

- ❖ 1 cup milk or almond milk
- ❖ 6 ounces Yoplait Original French Vanilla yogurt
- ❖ 1/2 teaspoon lime zest
- ❖ Juice of one large lime
- ❖ 1 cup fresh spinach
- ❖ 1 cup frozen blackberries
- ❖ 1 frozen banana

INSTRUCTIONS

1. Add milk, yogurt, lime zest, lime juice, spinach, blackberries, and banana to the blender. Place the lid on and blend until smooth. Pour into glasses and serve immediately.

2. Note-I always keeps unpeeled bananas in the freezer for smoothies. If you don't have a frozen banana, you can use a regular banana and add a few ice cubes.

34.PINEAPPLE COCONUT SMOOTHIE

INGREDIENTS

- ❖ 2 cups chopped fresh pineapple
- ❖ 1/2 cup coconut milk
- ❖ 6 oz Greek vanilla or coconut yogurt
- ❖ 2 tablespoons coconut
- ❖ 1 cup ice
- ❖ Toasted coconut, for garnish, optional

INSTRUCTIONS

1. Combine the pineapple, coconut milk, yogurt, coconut, and ice in a blender. Blend until smooth. Pour smoothie into two glasses and garnish with toasted coconut, if using. Serve immediately.

35.CHOCOLATE RASPBERRY SMOOTHIE

INGREDIENTS

- ❖ 1 cup Almond Breeze Chocolate Unsweetened Almond milk
- ❖ 1 medium frozen banana
- ❖ 1 cup frozen raspberries
- ❖ 2 tablespoons Dutch-processed cocoa powder
- ❖ Raspberries and sprinkles for serving, if desired

INSTRUCTIONS

1. Place all ingredients in a blender and blend until smooth. Serve immediately. Garnish with raspberries and sprinkles, if desired!
2. Note-we uses Almond Breeze Chocolate Unsweetened Almond milk, and I think it is plenty sweet. If you want a sweeter drink, you can use Almond Breeze regular Chocolate Almond milk.

36.RASPBERRY COCONUT SMOOTHIE

INGREDIENTS

- ❖ 1 cup Almond Breeze Unsweetened Almond Milk Coconut milk
- ❖ 1 cup raspberries fresh or frozen
- ❖ 1/2 medium banana
- ❖ 1/2 cup spinach
- ❖ -2 tablespoons coconut for garnish

INSTRUCTIONS

1. Place the milk, raspberries, banana, and spinach in the blender and blend until smooth. Pour into a glass and garnish with coconut. Serve immediately.
2. Note: I use fresh raspberries; I like to throw in a few ice cubes to get a thicker/colder smoothie.

37.GREEN SMOOTHIE BOWL

INGREDIENTS
- ❖ 1/2 frozen banana
- ❖ 1/2 cup frozen pineapple
- ❖ 1 cup kale
- ❖ 1/4 avocado
- ❖ 1/2 cup full-fat coconut milk canned
- ❖ toppings: banana pineapple, granola, chia seeds, unsweetened coconut

INSTRUCTIONS
1. Add all ingredients aside from toppings in the blender. Blend on high for 1-2 minutes until thick and smooth. If you don't have a high-powered blender, it may take a little longer.
2. Pour into a large bowl and add assorted toppings. Eat immediately.

38.MOCHA PROTEIN SMOOTHIE BOWL

INGREDIENTS

- ❖ 1 frozen banana
- ❖ 1/2 cup coconut milk canned and shaken well
- ❖ 1 teaspoon instant coffee granules
- ❖ 1/2 cup frozen cauliflower
- ❖ 1/4 avocado set or room temp
- ❖ 1 scoop chocolate protein powder
- ❖ 2 tablespoons unsweetened cocoa powder
- ❖ Optional toppings: banana slices unsweetened coconut, chia seeds, dark chocolate chips, granola

INSTRUCTIONS

1. Add all of the ingredients to a high-powered blender and blend on high for 1-2 minutes, or until the mixture is smooth and has no clumps.
2. Pour into a bowl and add your toppings if using. Eat immediately and enjoy!

39.DRAGONFRUIT SMOOTHIE PITAYA BOWL

INGREDIENTS

2 packs pitaya
- ❖ 1 frozen banana
- ❖ 1/2 cup frozen strawberries
- ❖ 1/2 cup dairy-free milk I used almond milk
- ❖ toppings: bananas, strawberries, nuts, granola, chia seeds, other fruit, and more!

INSTRUCTIONS

1. Add all ingredients aside from toppings in the blender. Blend on high for 1-2 minutes until thick and smooth. If you don't have a high-powered blender, it may take a little longer.
2. Pour into large bowls and add assorted toppings. Eat immediately.

40. TROPICAL COCONUT SMOOTHIE BOWL

INGREDIENTS

- ❖ 2 frozen bananas
- ❖ 1 1/2 cups frozen pineapple
- ❖ 1 cup frozen mango
- ❖ 1/2 cup coconut milk shaken
- ❖ 2 tablespoons honey omit for a vegan option
- ❖ 1/4 teaspoon coconut extract
- ❖ toppings: mango granola, chia seeds, cherries, other fruit,

INSTRUCTIONS

1. Add all ingredients aside from toppings in the blender. Blend on high for 1-2 minutes until thick and smooth. If you don't have a high-powered blender, it may take a little longer.
2. Pour into a large bowl and add assorted toppings. Eat immediately.

41.BERRY ALMOND SMOOTHIE BOWL

INGREDIENTS

- ❖ 1 1/2 cups frozen berry mixture
- ❖ 3 tablespoons almond butter
- ❖ 1 banana divided in half
- ❖ 1/4 cup unsweetened coconut
- ❖ 1/3 cup vanilla almond milk
- ❖ 1/8 cup chia seeds optional
- ❖ 1/8 cup muesli optional
- ❖ 1/8 cup dark chocolate chips optional

INSTRUCTIONS

1. Add the berries, almond margarine, half of the banana, coconut drops, and almond milk to the blender. Heartbeat until smooth. The combination will be thick. Spoon into an enormous bowl and top with cuts of other portions of banana, dull chocolate chips, muesli, extra coconut, and chia seeds.
2. Eat right away!

42.SIMPLE PALEO GRANOLA

INGREDIENTS

- ❖ ¼ cup coconut oil melted
- ❖ ⅓ cup pure maple syrup
- ❖ 1/3 cup creamy cashew butter
- ❖ 1 teaspoon cinnamon
- ❖ 2 teaspoons vanilla extract
- ❖ ½ teaspoon kosher salt
- ❖ 2 cups cashews roughly chopped
- ❖ 1 cup pecans roughly chopped
- ❖ 2 tablespoons chia seeds
- ❖ 2 tablespoons flaxseed
- ❖ 1 cup unsweetened coconut flakes

INSTRUCTIONS

1. Preheat the broiler to 300 degrees F and position a rack in the focal point of the stove.
2. In a large bowl, whisk together the softened coconut oil, maple syrup, cashew spread, cinnamon, vanilla, and salt. Add the cashews, walnuts, chia seeds, flaxseed, coconut chips, dried blueberries, and blend well to cover.
3. Pour and spread the blend equally onto a massive preparing sheet and heat for 45 minutes, mixing like clockwork to abstain from consuming.
4. When the granola is sautéed and done cooking, eliminate it from the stove and let cool totally to get fresh.
5. Store in a compartment with an impermeable seal, and it should keep for as long as 3 weeks.

43.TROPICALE SMOOTHIE

INGREDIENTS

- ❖ 1 cup coconut water
- ❖ 1 banana
- ❖ 1/2 cup frozen pineapple chunks
- ❖ 1/2 cup frozen mango chunks
- ❖ 1/2 cup frozen strawberries
- ❖ 1 cup kale leaves
- ❖ Handful of ice

INSTRUCTIONS

1. Spot all fixings into the blender, with the base's fluids at that point, mix until smooth and to your ideal consistency. On the off chance that excessively thick, add more fluid. If too slender, add some ice to thicken up or more frozen natural products.

44.RASPBERRY PEACH SPINACH SMOOTHIE

INGREDIENTS

- ❖ 1 1/3 cup unsweetened almond milk
- ❖ 1/3 cup plain kefir or plain Greek yogurt
- ❖ 3 pitted dates
- ❖ 2/3 cup frozen raspberries
- ❖ 3/4 cup frozen peach slices
- ❖ A giant handful of baby spinach leaves
- ❖ OPTIONAL ADD-INS
- ❖ 1 tablespoon hemp hearts
- ❖ 1 teaspoon bee pollen
- ❖ 1 teaspoon maca powder
- ❖ 1-2 tablespoons of your favorite nut butter

INSTRUCTIONS

1. Place all ingredients into the blender, with the liquids at the bottom, then blend until smooth and to your desired consistency. If too thick, add more liquid. If too thin, add some ice to thicken up or more frozen fruit.

45.BANANA PEANUT BUTTER AND DATE SMOOTHIE

INGREDIENTS

- ❖ 1 cup unsweetened plain almond milk
- ❖ 1 ripe banana
- ❖ 4-5 pitted dates
- ❖ 1 frozen banana
- ❖ 2 tablespoons natural creamy peanut butter
- ❖ 1/4 - 1/2 cup ice
- ❖ Optional: your favorite protein powder. I recommend vanilla or chocolate flavor, so it doesn't affect this smoothie's taste too much.

INSTRUCTIONS

1. Place all ingredients into a power blender (like a Vitamix) and blend until smooth. If you like it thinner, add more almond milk.

46.PITAYA SMOOTHIE BOWL

INGREDIENTS

- ❖ 1 cup almond milk
- ❖ 1 pitaya pack
- ❖ 2/3 cup frozen fruit (I used a mixture of pineapple peaches and mangoes)
- ❖ Optional toppings: almond butter, fresh fruit, coconut flakes, granola

INSTRUCTIONS

1. Add the almond milk, pitaya pack, and frozen fruit into a powerful blender. Blend until smooth. If you like your smoothie on the thicker side, add more frozen fruit. If you want your smoothie on the thinner side, add more almond milk/liquid.
2. Top with your favorite toppings.

47.MIXED BERRY SMOOTHIE BOWL

INGREDIENTS

- ❖ 1 cup coconut milk beverage, not from the can
- ❖ 2/3 cup frozen mixed berries
- ❖ 1 large banana
- ❖ 2 tablespoons cashew butter, or your favorite nut butter
- ❖ Your favorite toppings: fruit, granola, chia seeds, etc.

INSTRUCTIONS

1. Pour the coconut milk into the bottom of the blender jar. Then add the frozen berries, banana, and cashew butter on top. Securely place the lid on the pot and blend until no chunks remain. You may need to stop and stir it around if it's too thick.
2. Pour smoothie into a bowl and place toppings on top.

48.PEACHY GREEN SMOOTHIE

INGREDIENTS

- ❖ 2 cups coconut milk beverage, NOT the canned coconut milk
- ❖ 2 cups frozen sliced peaches
- ❖ 2 frozen underripe bananas, sliced
- ❖ 1 teaspoon grated fresh ginger, optional
- ❖ 2 cups loosely packed spinach leaves

INSTRUCTIONS

1. Pour the coconut milk into a blender and add the peaches, banana, ginger (if using), and spinach.
2. Blend until smooth.

49.GREEN MONSTER SMOOTHIE

INGREDIENTS

- ❖ 2 cups frozen fruit (I used mixed fruit that included pineapples grapes, strawberries, mangos, and peaches)
- ❖ 1 banana broken into pieces
- ❖ 1 1/2 cup almond milk
- ❖ Large handful of spinach

INSTRUCTIONS

1. Throw everything in the blender and blend until a smooth consistency. If it gets stuck, turn it off, and use a spatula to break it up and start it again.

50.LIGHTENED-UP DAIRY-FREE ORANGE SMOOTHIE

INGREDIENTS

- ❖ 6 frozen Trop50 ice cubes (approximately 3/4 cup)
- ❖ 1/2 cup full-fat coconut milk
- ❖ 1/3 cup unsweetened vanilla almond milk
- ❖ 1 orange, peeled (with any seeds removed) + zest
- ❖ Splash of vanilla extract

INSTRUCTIONS

1. Place all ingredients into a high-powdered blender.
2. Blend and enjoy!

CONCLUSION

Whether you're looking for a way to add some nutrition to your daily diet or seeking to learn more about smoothies to begin your first cleanse, you now have some excellent recipes and tips to get you started. Remember, though, to use this as a general guide. Once you get the hang of mixing flavors, feel free to make up your own blends to suit your tastes and health goals.

The Smoothie Recipe Book for Beginners

50 Smoothie Recipes

Jennifer Abrahams

All rights reserved.

Disclaimer

INTRODUCTION

A smoothie recipe is a drink made from pureed raw fruit and/or vegetables, using a blender. A smoothie often has a liquid base such as water, fruit juice, dairy products, such as milk, yogurt, ice cream or cottage cheese.

1.MINTY PINEAPPLE SMOOTHIE

INGREDIENTS

- ❖ 200g pineapple, peeled, cored and cut into chunks

- ❖ a few mints leave

- ❖ 50g baby spinach leaves

- ❖ 25g oats

- ❖ 2 tbsp linseed

- ❖ handful unsalted, unroasted cashew nuts

- ❖ fresh lime juice, to taste

INSTRUCTION

1. Put all the ingredients in a blender with 200ml water and process until smooth. If it's too thick, add more water (up to 400ml) until you get the right mix.

2.GREEN RAINBOW SMOOTHIE BOWL

INGREDIENTS

- ❖ 50g spinach
- ❖ 1 avocado, stoned, peeled and halved
- ❖ 1 ripe mango, stoned, peeled and cut into chunks
- ❖ 1 apple, cored and cut into chunks
- ❖ 200ml almond milk
- ❖ 1 dragon fruit, peeled and cut into even chunks
- ❖ 100g mixed berries (we used strawberries, raspberries and blueberries)

INSTRUCTION

1. Put the spinach, avocado, mango, apple and almond milk in a blender, and blitz until smooth and thick. Divide between two bowls and top with the dragon fruit and berries.

3.TROPICAL SMOOTHIE BOWL

INGREDIENTS

- ❖ 1 small ripe mango, stoned, peeled and cut into chunks

- ❖ 200g pineapple, peeled, cored and cut into chunks

- ❖ 2 ripe bananas

- ❖ 2 tbsp coconut yogurt (not coconut-flavored yogurt)

- ❖ 150ml coconut drinking milk

- ❖ 2 passion fruits, halved, seeds scooped out

- ❖ handful blueberries

- ❖ 2 tbsp coconut flakes

- ❖ a few mint leaves

INSTRUCTIONS

1. Put the mango, pineapple, bananas, yogurt and coconut milk in a blender, and blitz until smooth and thick. Pour into two bowls and decorate with the passion fruit, blueberries, coconut flakes and mint leaves. Will keep in the fridge for 1 day. Add the toppings just before serving.

4.TURMERIC SMOOTHIE BOWL

INGREDIENTS

- ❖ 10cm/4in fresh turmeric, or 2 tsp ground turmeric

- ❖ 3 tbsp coconut milk yogurt (we used Co Yoh), or the cream skimmed from the top of canned coconut milk

- ❖ 50g gluten-free oats

- ❖ 1 tbsp cashew butter (or a handful of cashews)

- ❖ 2 bananas, peeled and roughly chopped

- ❖ ½ tsp ground cinnamon

- ❖ 1 tbsp chia seeds or chopped nuts, to serve

INSTRUCTION

1. Peel the turmeric root, if using, and grate. Put all ingredients in a blender with 600ml water and blend until smooth. Serve in a bowl with chia seeds or some chopped nuts sprinkled over.

5. CREAMY MANGO & COCONUT SMOOTHIE

INGREDIENTS

- ❖ 200ml (½ tall glass) coconut milk (we used Kara Dairy Free)

- ❖ 4 tbsp coconut milk yogurt (we used Coyo)

- ❖ 1 banana

- ❖ 1 tbsp ground flaxseed, sunflower and pumpkin seed (we used Linwood's)

- ❖ 120g (¼ bag) frozen mango chunks

- ❖ 1 passion fruit, to finish (optional)

INSTRUCTION

1. Measure all the ingredients or use a tall glass for speed – they don't have to be exact. Put them into a blender and blitz until smooth. Pour into 1 tall glass (you'll have enough for a top up) or two short tumblers. Cut the passion fruit in half, if using, and scrape the seeds on top.

6.SUPER BERRY SMOOTHIE

INGREDIENTS

- ❖ 450g bag frozen berry
- ❖ 450g pot fat-free strawberry yogurt
- ❖ 100ml milk
- ❖ 25g porridge oat
- ❖ 2 tsp honey (optional)

INSTRUCTION

1. Whizz the berries, yogurt and milk together with a stick blender until smooth. Stir through the porridge oats, then pour into 4 glasses and serve with a drizzle of honey, if you like.

7.BLACKBERRY & BEETROOT SMOOTHIE

INGREDIENTS

- ❖ 250ml coconut water
- ❖ pinch ground cinnamon
- ❖ ¼ tsp ground nutmeg
- ❖ 4cm piece fresh ginger, peeled
- ❖ 1 tbsp shelled hemp seeds
- ❖ 2 small cooked beetroot, roughly chopped
- ❖ small handful blackberries
- ❖ 1 pear, roughly chopped
- ❖ small handful kale

INSTRUCTION

1. Add the coconut water to your blender with the spices and fresh ginger. Tip in the remaining ingredients and blend until smooth. Add more liquid if you prefer a thinner consistency. Pour into glasses and serve.

8.VITAMIN BOOSTER SMOOTHIE

INGREDIENTS

- ❖ 1 orange, peeled and roughly chopped
- ❖ 1 large carrot, peeled and roughly chopped
- ❖ 2 sticks celery, roughly chopped
- ❖ 50g mango, roughly chopped
- ❖ 200ml water
- ❖ Method

INSTRUCTION

1. Put all the orange, carrot, celery and mango in the blender, top up with water, then blitz until smooth.

9.BERRY SMOOTHIE CUBES

INGREDIENTS

- ❖ blackberries
- ❖ strawberries
- ❖ raspberries, passion fruit
- ❖ mango
- ❖ any other fruits you like

INSTRUCTION

1. Purée a fruit (try blackberries, strawberries, raspberries, passion fruit and mango, in a food processor, leave pips in or sieve.

2. Freeze in ice trays ready to whizz up (3 per serving) with a banana, 150ml pot plain yogurt, and milk and honey to taste.

10.PEACH MELBA SMOOTHIE

INGREDIENTS

- ❖ 410g can peach halves
- ❖ 100g frozen raspberry, plus a few for garnish
- ❖ 100ml orange juice
- ❖ 150ml fresh custard, plus a spoonful for garnish

INSTRUCTION

1. Drain and rinse peaches and place in a blender with raspberries. Add orange juice and fresh custard and whizz together.

2. Pour over ice, garnish with another spoonful of custard and a few raspberries. Best served chilled.

11.BANANA, CLEMENTINE & MANGO SMOOTHIE

INGREDIENTS

- ❖ about 24 juicy clementine, plus an extra one for decoration

- ❖ 2 small, very ripe and juicy mangoes

- ❖ 2 ripe bananas

- ❖ 500g tub whole milk or low-fat yogurt

- ❖ handful of ice cubes (optional)

INSTRUCTION

1. Halve the clementine and squeeze out the juice – you should have about 600ml/1 pint. (This can be done the night before.) Peel the mangoes, slice the fruit away from the stone in the Centre, then chop the flesh into rough pieces. Peel and slice the bananas.

2. Put the clementine juice, mango flesh, bananas, yogurt and ice cubes into a liquidizer and blend until smooth. Pour into six glasses and serve. (You might need to make this in two batches, depending on the size of your liquidizer.) If you don't add ice cubes, chill in the fridge until ready to serve.

12.AÇAÍ SMOOTHIE

INGREDIENTS

- ❖ 100g raw, frozen, unsweetened açai pulp, thawed

- ❖ 50g frozen pineapple

- ❖ 100g strawberry

- ❖ 1 medium banana

- ❖ 250ml mango or orange juice

- ❖ 1 tbsp agave nectar or honey

INSTRUCTION

1. Place all ingredients in the blender or a food processor. Blend until smooth. If it's too thick add a bit more mango or orange juice. Serve in 2 tall glasses.

13.MANGO & PASSION FRUIT SMOOTHIE

INGREDIENTS

- ❖ 400g/14oz peeled and chopped ripe mango

- ❖ 2 x 125g pots fat-free mango yogurt

- ❖ 250ml skimmed milk

- ❖ juice 1 lime

- ❖ 4 passion fruits, halved

INSTRUCTION

1. Whizz the mango, yogurt and milk together in a blender until smooth. Stir in the lime juice, then pour into 4 glasses. Scoop the pulp of a passion fruit into each one, and swirl before serving.

14.FOREST FRUIT & BANANA SMOOTHIE

INGREDIENTS

- ❖ frozen fruits of the forest

- ❖ banana, sliced

- ❖ low-fat fruits of the forest yogurt

INSTRUCTION

1. Whizz frozen fruits of the forest and sliced banana in a food processor with low-fat fruits of the forest yogurt.

15.SMOOTHIE JELLIES WITH ICE CREAM

INGREDIENTS

- ❖ 6 sheets leaf gelatin

- ❖ 1l bottle orange, mango and passion fruit smoothie (we used Innocent)

- ❖ To serve

- ❖ 500ml tub good-quality vanilla ice cream such as Green & Black's (you might not need it all)

INSTRUCTION

1. Put the leaf gelatin into a bowl and cover with cold water. Leave for a few mins until soft and floppy. Meanwhile, gently heat the smoothie in a saucepan without boiling. Take off the heat. Lift the gelatin out of the water, squeeze out the excess water, then add it to the smoothie pan. Stir well until smooth, then pour into 12 moulds, pots or glasses, or use 24 shot-glass-sized pots. Chill for at least 1 hour to set.

2. For perfect mini scoops of ice cream, dip a tbsp measuring spoon into a cup of hot water, then shake off the excess. Scoop the ice cream, dipping the spoon in the hot water each time. Serve each smoothie jelly topped with ice cream.

16.BANANA, HONEY & HAZELNUT SMOOTHIE

INGREDIENTS

- ❖ 1 peeled, sliced banana

- ❖ 250ml soya milk

- ❖ 1 tsp honey

- ❖ a little grated nutmeg

- ❖ 2 tsp chopped hazelnuts, to serve

INSTRUCTION

1. Blend the banana with soya milk, honey and a little grated nutmeg until smooth. Pour into two large glasses and top with the toasted, chopped hazelnuts to serve.

17.BREAKFAST SUPER-SHAKE

INGREDIENTS

- ❖ 100ml full-fat milk
- ❖ 2 tbsp natural yogurt
- ❖ 1 banana
- ❖ 150g frozen fruits of the forest
- ❖ 50g blueberries
- ❖ 1 tbsp chia seeds
- ❖ ½ tsp cinnamon
- ❖ 1 tbsp goji berries
- ❖ 1 tsp mixed seeds
- ❖ 1 tsp honey (ideally Manuka)

INSTRUCTION

1. Put the ingredients in a blender and blitz until smooth. Pour into a glass and enjoy!

18.ALMOND MILK

INGREDIENTS

- ❖ 150g whole almonds

INSTRUCTION

1. Put the almonds in a large bowl and cover with water, then cover the bowl and leave to soak overnight or for at least 4 hrs.

2. The next day, drain and rinse the almonds, then tip into a blender with 750ml cold water. Whizz until smooth. Pour the mixture into a muslin-lined sieve over a jug and allow it to drip through. Stir the mixture gently with a spoon to speed up the process.

3. When most of the liquid has gone through into the jug, gather the sides of the muslin together and squeeze tightly with both hands to extract the last of the milk.

19.EASY CHOCOLATE FUDGE CAKE

INGREDIENTS

- ❖ 150ml sunflower oil, plus extra for the tin
- ❖ 175g self-rising flour
- ❖ 2 tbsp cocoa powder
- ❖ 1 tsp bicarbonate of soda
- ❖ 150g caster sugar
- ❖ 2 tbsp golden syrup
- ❖ 2 large eggs, lightly beaten
- ❖ 150ml semi-skimmed milk

For the icing

- ❖ 100g unsalted butter
- ❖ 225g icing sugar
- ❖ 40g cocoa powder
- ❖ 2½ tbsp milk (a little more if needed)

INSTRUCTION

1. Heat the oven to 180C/160C fan/gas 4. Oil and line the base of two 18cm sandwich tins. Sieve the flour, cocoa powder and bicarbonate of soda into a bowl. Add the caster sugar and mix well.

2. Make a well in the Centre and add the golden syrup, eggs, sunflower oil and milk. Beat well with an electric whisk until smooth.

3. Pour the mixture into the two tins and bake for 25-30 mins until risen and firm to the touch. Remove from oven, leave to cool for 10 mins before turning out onto a cooling rack.

4. To make the icing, beat the unsalted butter in a bowl until soft. Gradually sieve and beat in the icing sugar and cocoa powder, then add enough of the milk to make the icing fluffy and spreadable.

5. Sandwich the two cakes together with the butter icing and cover the sides and the top of the cake with more icing.

20.FAUX GRAS WITH TOAST & PICKLES

INGREDIENTS

- ❖ 100g butter, softened

- ❖ 300g organic chicken or duck livers, trimmed, cleaned and patted dry

To serve

- ❖ sliced brioche or sourdough

- ❖ cornichons

- ❖ chutney

- ❖ sea salt flakes

INSTRUCTION

1. Heat 50g butter in a frying pan until sizzling, add the livers and fry for 4 mins until colored on the outside and slightly pink in the middle. Leave to cool, then tip the contents of the pan into a food processor or a smoothie bullet blender. Season generously with salt and add the remaining butter. Blitz until you have a smooth purée, then scrape into a container, smooth over the top and place in the fridge to chill for at least 2 hrs. Can be made a day ahead.

2. To serve, griddle slices of brioche or sourdough, and tip some cornichons and chutney into small pots. Put a large spoon in a cup of hot water. As if serving ice cream, scoop a spoonful of the faux

gras onto each plate, dipping the spoon into the water after each scoop. Sprinkle a few salt flakes over each scoop and serve with the toasts, cornichons and chutney.

21.STRAWBERRY ACAI SMOOTHIE

INGREDIENTS

- ❖ oz packet frozen acai
- ❖ 1 banana
- ❖ 1 cup strawberries
- ❖ 3/4 cup almond milk or cashew milk

INSTRUCTIONS

1. Add all ingredients to a high-powered blender and blend until smooth.

22.POST WORKOUT GREEN SMOOTHIE

INGREDIENTS

- ❖ 2 cups filtered water

- ❖ 2 cups baby spinach

- ❖ 1 banana, sliced and frozen

- ❖ 1 green apple

- ❖ 1/4 avocado

- ❖ 2 tbsp collagen powder

- ❖ 2 tbsp protein powder

- ❖ 2 tbsp chia seeds

INSTRUCTIONS

1. Place all ingredients into a high-powered blender.

2. Blend for 30 seconds or until smooth.

23.SPICED PERSIMMON SMOOTHIE

INGREDIENTS

- ❖ 2 ripe Fuyu persimmons
- ❖ 1 banana, frozen
- ❖ 1 cup almond milk, cashew milk or another nut milk
- ❖ 1/4 tsp ginger
- ❖ 1/4 tsp cinnamon
- ❖ pinch of ground cloves

INSTRUCTIONS

1. Wash the persimmons and slice off the stem. Add them along with all other ingredients to a high-powered blender and blend for one minute.

2. Optionally, garnish the inside of a glass with a thin persimmon slice.

24.GOLDEN BEET, CARROT AND TURMERIC SMOOTHIE

INGREDIENTS

- ❖ 2 golden beets, chopped
- ❖ 1 large carrot, chopped
- ❖ 1 banana, peeled, sliced and frozen
- ❖ 4 mandarin oranges, peeled
- ❖ 1 lemon, juiced
- ❖ 1/4 tsp turmeric powder
- ❖ 1 1/2 cup cold water

OPTIONAL TOPPING

- ❖ grated carrot
- ❖ hemp seeds

INSTRUCTIONS

1. Add all ingredients into a high-powered blender and blend until smooth.

2. Pour into glasses and add any optional toppings

25.CHOCOLATE COLLAGEN SMOOTHIE

INGREDIENTS

- ❖ 2 cups coconut milk, or other milk

- ❖ 1 frozen banana

- ❖ 2 tbsp almond butter

- ❖ 1/4 cup raw cacao powder

- ❖ 2 scoops, or more Vital Proteins Collagen Peptides

INSTRUCTIONS

1. Add all ingredients to a high-powered blender and blend until smooth.

26.CASHEW DATE SHAKE (VEGAN, PALEO)

INGREDIENTS

- ❖ 2/3 cup raw cashews, soaked for 2-4 hours
- ❖ 6 Medjool dates, pitted and soaked for 10 minutes
- ❖ 1 banana, sliced and frozen
- ❖ 3/4 cup water
- ❖ 2 cups ice
- ❖ 1 tsp vanilla extract
- ❖ 1/4 tsp nutmeg
- ❖ pinch cinnamon
- ❖ pinch sea salt

INSTRUCTIONS

1. Once your cashews and dates have been soaked and drained add them to a high-powered blender. Add the remaining ingredients and blend on high until thick and creamy.

27.DARK CHERRY SMOOTHIE BOWL

INGREDIENTS

- ❖ cups frozen cherries, pitted
- ❖ 1 banana
- ❖ 1/2 cup coconut water

OPTIONAL TOPPING

- ❖ whole cherries
- ❖ coconut flakes
- ❖ sliced almonds
- ❖ raw cacao nibs

INSTRUCTIONS

1. Add the frozen cherries, banana and coconut water into a high-powered blender. Blend until smooth.

2. Pour the smoothie mixture into a bowl and add the toppings.

28.PITAYA SMOOTHIE BOWL

INGREDIENTS

- ❖ 2 Pitaya Plus packs
- ❖ 1 banana
- ❖ 4 strawberries
- ❖ 3/4 cup coconut water

OPTIONAL TOPPINGS

- ❖ strawberries
- ❖ kiwi fruit
- ❖ cashews
- ❖ coconut

INSTRUCTIONS

1. Add the frozen pitaya, banana, strawberries and coconut water into a high powered blender. Blend on high for one minute, until well combined.

2. Pour your pitaya smoothie into a bowl and add your toppings.

29.HEALTHY COCOA, BANANA, PB SMOOTHIE

INGREDIENTS

- ❖ 1 cup milk

- ❖ ½ chopped frozen banana, or more to taste

- ❖ 2 tablespoons peanut butter

- ❖ 2 teaspoons unsweetened cocoa powder

- ❖ 1 teaspoon honey

INSTRUCTION

1. Blend milk, banana, peanut butter, cocoa powder, and honey together in a blender until smooth.

30.TURMERIC LATTE

INGREDIENTS

- ❖ 1 cup unsweetened almond milk or coconut milk beverage

- ❖ 1 tablespoon grated fresh turmeric

- ❖ 2 teaspoons pure maple syrup or honey

- ❖ 1 teaspoon grated fresh ginger

- ❖ Pinch of ground pepper

- ❖ 1 pinch Ground cinnamon for garnish

INSTRUCTIONS

1. Combine milk, turmeric, maple syrup (or honey), ginger and pepper in a blender. Process on high until very smooth, about 1 minute. Pour into a small saucepan and heat over medium-high heat until steaming hot but not boiling. Transfer to a mug. Garnish with a sprinkle of cinnamon, if desired.

31.FRUIT & YOGURT SMOOTHIE

INGREDIENTS

- ❖ 3/4 cup nonfat plain yogurt

- ❖ 1/2 cup 100% pure fruit juice

- ❖ 1 1/2 cups (6 1/2 ounces) frozen fruit, such as blueberries, raspberries, pineapple or peaches

INSTRUCTIONS

1. Puree yogurt with juice in a blender until smooth. With the motor running, add fruit through the hole in the lid and continue to puree until smooth.

32.UNICORN SMOOTHIE

INGREDIENTS

- 1 ½ cups low-fat milk, divided
- 1 ½ cups low-fat vanilla yogurt, divided
- 3 large bananas, divided
- 1 cup frozen blackberries or blueberries
- 1 cup frozen mango chunks
- 1 cup frozen raspberries or strawberries
- Star fruit, kiwi, mixed berries and chia seeds for garnish

INSTRUCTION

1. Combine 1/2 cup each milk and yogurt, 1 banana and blackberries (or blueberries) in a blender. Blend until smooth. Divide the mixture among 4 large glasses. Place in the freezer. Rinse out the blender.

2. Combine 1/2 cup each milk and yogurt, 1 banana and mango chunks in the blender. Blend until smooth. Divide the mixture over the purple layer in the glasses. Return the glasses to the freezer. Rinse out the blender.

3. Combine the remaining 1/2 cup each milk and yogurt, the remaining banana and raspberries (or strawberries) in the blender. Blend until smooth. Divide the mixture over the yellow layer

in the glasses. Run a skewer around the edges to swirl the layers slightly.

4. If desired, arrange star fruit slices, kiwi slices and berries on 4 wooden skewers to garnish each glass. Sprinkle with chia seeds, if desired.

33.CHOCOLATE-BANANA PROTEIN SMOOTHIE

INGREDIENTS

- ❖ 1 banana, frozen
- ❖ ½ cup cooked red lentils
- ❖ ½ cup nonfat milk
- ❖ 2 teaspoons unsweetened cocoa powder
- ❖ 1 teaspoon pure maple syrup

DIRECTIONS

1. Combine banana, lentils, milk, cocoa and syrup in a blender.

2. Puree until smooth.

34.CREAMSICLE BREAKFAST SMOOTHIE

INGREDIENTS

- ❖ 1 cup cold pure coconut water, without added sugar or flavor (see Tip)

- ❖ 1 cup nonfat vanilla Greek yogurt

- ❖ 1 cup frozen or fresh mango chunks

- ❖ 3 tablespoons frozen orange juice concentrate

- ❖ 2 cups ice

DIRECTIONS

1. Blend coconut water, yogurt, mango, orange juice concentrate and ice in a blender until smooth.

35.BERRY-COCONUT SMOOTHIE

INGREDIENTS

- ❖ ½ cup cooked red lentils (see Tips), cooled

- ❖ ¾ cup unsweetened vanilla coconut milk beverage

- ❖ ½ cup frozen mixed berries

- ❖ ½ cup frozen sliced banana

- ❖ 1 tablespoon unsweetened shredded coconut, plus more for garnish

- ❖ 1 teaspoon honey

- ❖ 3 ice cubes

DIRECTIONS

1. Place lentils, coconut milk, berries, banana, coconut, honey and ice cubes in a blender. Blend on high until very smooth, 2 to 3 minutes. Garnish with more coconut, if desired.

36.CARROT SMOOTHIE

INGREDIENTS

- ❖ 1 cup sliced carrots
- ❖ ½ teaspoon finely shredded orange peel
- ❖ 1 cup orange juice
- ❖ 1 ½ cups ice cubes
- ❖ 3 (1 inch) pieces Orange peel curls

DIRECTIONS

1. In a covered small saucepan, cook carrots in a small amount of boiling water about 15 minutes or until very tender. Drain well. Cool.

2. Place drained carrots in a blender. Add finely shredded orange peel and orange juice. Cover and blend until smooth. Add ice cubes; cover and blend until smooth. Pour into glasses. If desired, garnish with orange peel curls.

37.HONEYDEW SMOOTHIE BOWL

INGREDIENTS

- ❖ 4 cups frozen cubed honeydew (1/2-inch pieces)

- ❖ ½ cup unsweetened coconut milk beverage

- ❖ ⅓ cup green juice, such as wheatgrass

- ❖ 1 tablespoon honey

- ❖ Pinch of salt

- ❖ Melon balls, berries, nuts and/or fresh basil for garnish

INSTRUCTIONS

1. Combine honeydew, coconut milk, juice, honey and salt in a food processor or high-speed blender. Alternate between pulsing and blending, stopping to stir and scrape down the sides as needed, until thick and smooth, 1 to 2 minutes. Serve the smoothie topped with more melon, berries, nuts and/or basil, if desired.

38.PEANUT BUTTER & JELLY SMOOTHIE

INGREDIENTS

- ❖ ½ cup low-fat milk

- ❖ ⅓ cup nonfat plain Greek yogurt

- ❖ 1 cup baby spinach

- ❖ 1 cup frozen banana slices (about 1 medium banana)

- ❖ ½ cup frozen strawberries

- ❖ 1 tablespoon natural peanut butter

- ❖ 1-2 teaspoons pure maple syrup or honey (optional)

INSTRUCTIONS

1. Add milk and yogurt to a blender, then add spinach, banana, strawberries, peanut butter and sweetener (if using); blend until smooth.

39.CANTALOUPE SMOOTHIE BOWL

INGREDIENTS

- ❖ 4 cups frozen cubed cantaloupe (1/2-inch pieces)

- ❖ ¾ cup carrot juice

- ❖ Pinch of salt

- ❖ Melon balls, berries, nuts and/or fresh basil for garnish

INSTRUCTIONS

1. Combine cantaloupe, juice and salt in a food processor or high-speed blender. Alternate between pulsing and blending, stopping to stir and scrape down the sides as needed, until thick and smooth, 1 to 2 minutes. Serve the smoothie topped with more melon, berries, nuts and/or basil, if desired.

40.JASON MRAZ'S AVOCADO GREEN SMOOTHIE

INGREDIENTS

- ❖ 1 ¼ cups cold unsweetened almond milk or coconut milk beverage

- ❖ 1 ripe avocado

- ❖ 1 ripe banana

- ❖ 1 sweet apple, such as Honeycrisp, sliced

- ❖ ½ large or 1 small stalk celery, chopped

- ❖ 2 cups lightly packed kale leaves or spinach

- ❖ 1 1-inch piece peeled fresh ginger

- ❖ 8 ice cubes

INSTRUCTIONS

1. Blend milk beverage, avocado, banana, apple, celery, kale (or spinach), ginger and ice in a blender until very smooth.

41.TOFU TROPIC SMOOTHIE

INGREDIENTS

- ❖ 2 cups diced frozen mango
- ❖ 1 ½ cups pineapple juice
- ❖ ¾ cup silken tofu
- ❖ ¼ cup lime juice
- ❖ 1 teaspoon freshly grated lime zest

INSTRUCTIONS

1. Combine mango, pineapple juice, tofu, lime juice and lime zest in a blender; blend until smooth. Serve immediately.

42.GOOD GREEN TEA SMOOTHIE

INGREDIENTS

- ❖ 3 cups frozen white grapes

- ❖ 2 packed cups baby spinach

- ❖ 1 1/2 cups strong brewed green tea (see Tip), cooled

- ❖ 1 medium ripe avocado

- ❖ 2 teaspoons honey

INSTRUCTIONS

1. Combine grapes, spinach, green tea, avocado and honey in a blender; blend until smooth. Serve immediately.

43.ORANGE FLAX SMOOTHIE

INGREDIENTS

- ❖ 2 cups frozen peach slices
- ❖ 1 cup carrot juice
- ❖ 1 cup orange juice
- ❖ 2 tablespoons ground flaxseed (see Tip)
- ❖ 1 tablespoon chopped fresh ginger

INSTRUCTIONS

1. Combine peaches, carrot juice, orange juice, flaxseed and ginger in blender; blend until smooth. Serve immediately.

44.MERMAID SMOOTHIE BOWL

INGREDIENTS

- ❖ 2 frozen bananas, peeled
- ❖ 2 kiwis, peeled
- ❖ 1 cup fresh pineapple chunks
- ❖ 1 cup unsweetened almond milk
- ❖ 2 teaspoons blue spirulina powder
- ❖ ½ cup fresh blueberries
- ❖ ½ small Fuji apple, thinly sliced and cut into 1-inch flower shapes

INSTRUCTIONS

1. Combine bananas, kiwis, pineapple, almond milk and spirulina in a blender. Blend on high until smooth, about 2 minutes.

2. Divide the smoothie between 2 bowls. Top with blueberries and apples.

45.ALMOND-MATCHA GREEN SMOOTHIE BOWL

INGREDIENTS

- ❖ ½ cup frozen sliced banana
- ❖ ½ cup frozen sliced peaches
- ❖ 1 cup fresh spinach
- ❖ ½ cup unsweetened almond milk
- ❖ 5 tablespoons slivered almonds, divided
- ❖ 1 ½ teaspoons matcha tea powder
- ❖ 1 teaspoon maple syrup
- ❖ ½ ripe kiwi, diced

INSTRUCTIONS

1. Blend banana, peaches, spinach, almond milk, 3 tablespoons almonds, matcha and maple syrup in a blender until very smooth.

2. Pour the smoothie into a bowl and top with kiwi and the remaining 2 tablespoons slivered almonds.

46.UNICORN SMOOTHIE

INGREDIENTS

- ❖ 1 ½ cups low-fat milk, divided

- ❖ 1 ½ cups low-fat vanilla yogurt, divided

- ❖ 3 large bananas, divided

- ❖ 1 cup frozen blackberries or blueberries

- ❖ 1 cup frozen mango chunks

- ❖ 1 cup frozen raspberries or strawberries

- ❖ Star fruit, kiwi, mixed berries and chia seeds for garnish

INSTRUCTIONS

1. Combine 1/2 cup each milk and yogurt, 1 banana and blackberries (or blueberries) in a blender. Blend until smooth. Divide the mixture among 4 large glasses. Place in the freezer. Rinse out the blender.

2. Combine 1/2 cup each milk and yogurt, 1 banana and mango chunks in the blender. Blend until smooth. Divide the mixture over the purple layer in the glasses. Return the glasses to the freezer. Rinse out the blender.

3. Combine the remaining 1/2 cup each milk and yogurt, the remaining banana and raspberries (or strawberries) in the blender. Blend until smooth. Divide the mixture over the yellow layer

in the glasses. Run a skewer around the edges to swirl the layers slightly.

4. If desired, arrange star fruit slices, kiwi slices and berries on 4 wooden skewers to garnish each glass. Sprinkle with chia seeds, if desired.

47.TRIPLE MELON SMOOTHIE

INGREDIENTS

- ❖ ½ cup chopped watermelon
- ❖ ½ cup chopped ripe cantaloupe
- ❖ ½ cup chopped ripe honeydew melon
- ❖ ¼ cup diced avocado
- ❖ 6 ice cubes
- ❖ Squeeze of lime juice

INSTRUCTIONS

1. Combine watermelon, cantaloupe, honeydew, avocado, ice and lime juice in a blender. Puree until smooth.

48.CITRUS BERRY SMOOTHIE

INGREDIENTS

- ❖ 1 ¼ cups fresh berries
- ❖ ¾ cup low-fat plain yogurt
- ❖ ½ cup orange juice
- ❖ 2 tablespoons nonfat dry milk
- ❖ 1 tablespoon toasted wheat germ
- ❖ 1 tablespoon honey
- ❖ ½ teaspoon vanilla extract

INSTRUCTIONS

1. Place berries, yogurt, orange juice, dry milk, wheat germ, honey and vanilla in a blender and blend until smooth.

49.WATERMELON-TURMERIC SMOOTHIE

INGREDIENTS

- ❖ 4 cups watermelon chunks, seeded
- ❖ ½ cup water
- ❖ 3 tablespoons lemon juice
- ❖ 3 tablespoons coarsely chopped peeled fresh ginger
- ❖ 3 tablespoons coarsely chopped peeled fresh turmeric (see Tip) or 1 teaspoon ground
- ❖ 4 teaspoons honey
- ❖ 1 teaspoon extra-virgin coconut oil
- ❖ ground pepper

INSTRUCTIONS

1. Combine watermelon, water, lemon juice, ginger, turmeric, honey, oil and pepper in a blender. Puree until smooth, about 1 minute.

50.REALLY GREEN SMOOTHIE

INGREDIENTS

- ❖ 1 large ripe banana
- ❖ 1 cup packed baby kale or coarsely chopped mature kale
- ❖ 1 cup unsweetened vanilla almond milk
- ❖ ¼ ripe avocado
- ❖ 1 tablespoon chia seeds
- ❖ 2 teaspoons honey
- ❖ 1 cup ice cubes

INSTRUCTIONS

1. Combine banana, kale, almond milk, avocado, chia seeds and honey in a blender. Blend on high until creamy and smooth. Add ice and blend until smooth.

CONCLUSION

Whether you're looking for a way to add some nutrition to your daily diet or seeking to learn more about smoothies to begin your first cleanse, you now have some excellent recipes and tips to get you started. Remember, though, to use this as a general guide. Once you get the hang of mixing flavors, feel free to make up your own blends to suit your tastes and health goals.

CPSIA information can be obtained
at www.ICGtesting.com
Printed in the USA
BVHW091252240521
608000BV00001B/15